JAMBA'S
Blending!

150+ DELICIOUS & HEALTHY RECIPES

D1372395

Pascoe Publishing, Inc.
Rocklin, California

Although every precaution has been taken in the preparation of this book, the publisher and authors assume no responsibility for errors or omissions, and make no representations or warranties with respect to the accuracy or completeness of the contents of this work and specifically disclaim all warranties, including without limitation warranties of fitness for a particular purpose. No liability is assumed for damages resulting from the use of the information contained herein, and no warranty may be created or extended by sales or promotional materials. Although every effort has been made to ensure that the information contained in this book is complete and accurate, neither the publisher nor the authors are engaged in rendering professional advice or services to the individual reader. This information is intended for entertainment purposes only. Nothing herein is intended as medical advice. It is not intended to replace the advice of a medical practitioner. Consumers should always consult with a health care professional prior to making changes to their diet or lifestyle, including any new eating programs. Neither the publisher nor authors shall be held responsible for any loss or damage allegedly arising from any information or suggestion in this book. The opinions expressed in this book represent the personal views of the authors and not that of the publisher or Jamba Juice Company.

Nutritional Analyses: Calculations for the nutritional analyses in this book are based on the largest number of servings listed within the recipes. Calculations are rounded up to the nearest gram or milligram, as appropriate. If two options for an ingredient are listed, the first one is used. Not included are optional ingredients or serving suggestions.

Cover & Interior Page Design: KB Design

Photography: Haystack-Media, an imprint of Pascoe Publishing, Inc.

Published in the United States of America by

Pascoe Publishing, Inc.
Rocklin, California
www.pascoepublishing.com

ISBN: 9781-929862-50-452895

10   9   8   7   6   5   4   3   2   1

Printed in China

Table of Contents

Table of Contents

Chapter 1

Introducing Jamba Juice®

Summer
Strawberry Soup,
page 119

Introduction & About Jamba Juice®

For Jamba Juice®, it's simple—real food tastes better and makes eating healthier easy. We started as a fruitful idea that took root in a small store in the beach town of San Luis Obispo, California back in 1990. The inspiration was to take the best that nature had to offer and make wholesome nutrition accessible to everyone by keeping it delicious, fun and simple. And from this pure and simple beginning, our commitment to your health and happiness continues to fuel us.

Our philosophy: when you put truly good, straight-from-the-earth ingredients into your body, you become a better you. And a better you makes a better world. At Jamba Juice® we blend whole foods with a higher purpose. We create blends full of goodness that get you moving and inspire you to pass that goodness along to the world.

Inside the pages of this book, you'll find recipes to inspire your own blended creations using the Jamba® Professional Blender. From veggie smoothies and whole fruit juices to herb-rich sauces and delicate baked goods, each recipe offers fresh ingredients, vibrant flavors and easy blending steps. Get in and out of the kitchen effortlessly—experience Jamba Juice® and BLEND IN THE GOOD™.

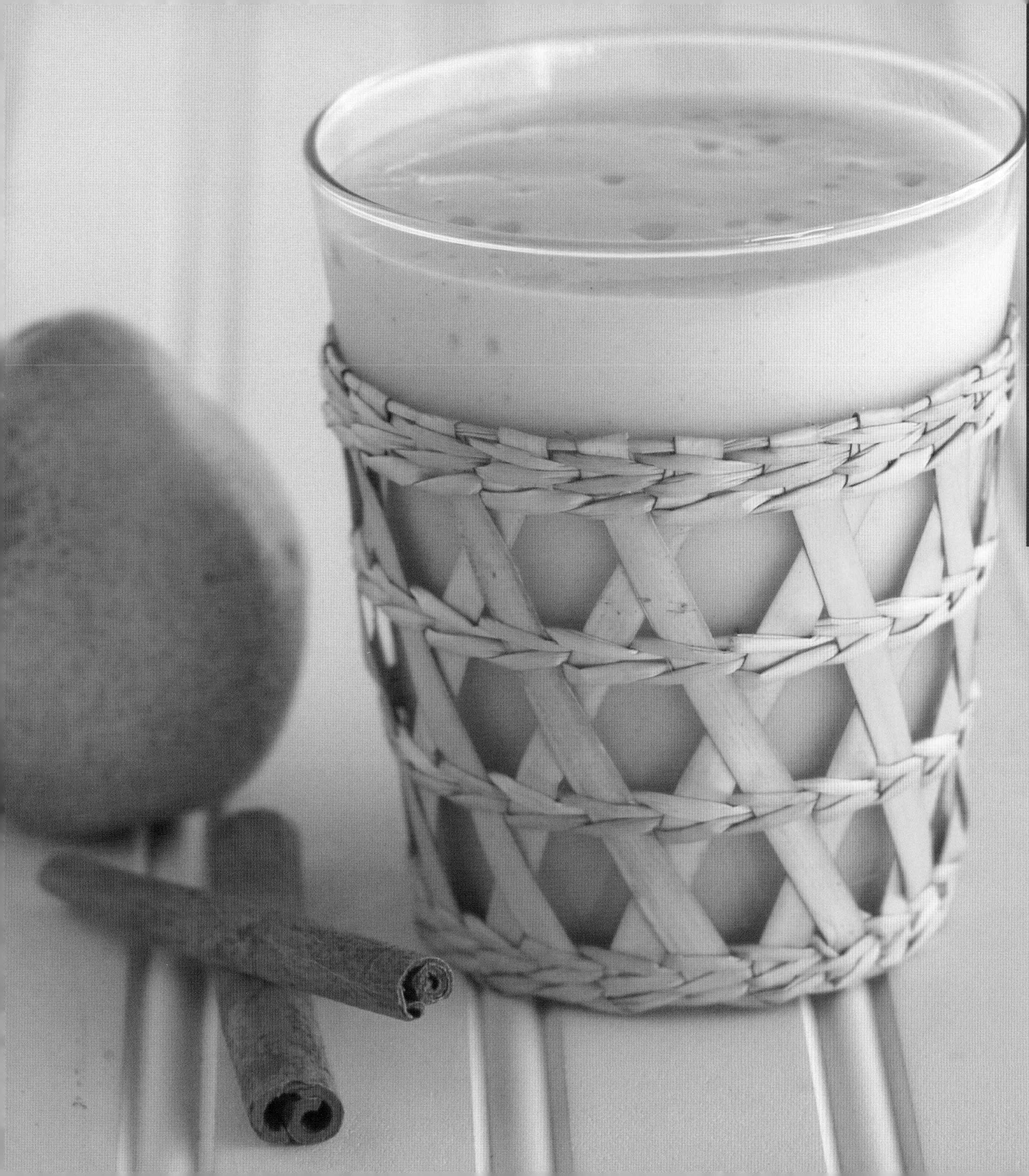

Blender Program Settings

Many blenders feature program settings to make blending easier. We've designed this book to accommodate a variety of higher performance blenders. If your blender features programs, look for the following symbols on the recipes. If the recipe reaches the smoothness or consistency of your liking before the program ends, simply press the Start Stop button to stop the cycle early. Depending on the recipe, ingredients, and desired consistency, you may even want to blend a little longer.

Smoothie

SMOOTHIE programs are perfect for blending frozen or fresh smoothies. For best results, add liquid ingredients first, then add fruit or vegetables. Ice and other frozen ingredients should be placed in the jar last.

Soup

Instead of heating soup ingredients on the stovetop, some blenders will feature a hot SOUP program. The SOUP setting purées and heats ingredients to just under the boiling point. When making soups, start with cold or room temperature ingredients.

Whole Juice

WHOLE JUICE setting gives a smooth, creamy consistency to puréed fruit or vegetables and a fine texture when whole grains or seeds are included in the juice recipe. It is great for blending more fibrous fruits and vegetables into a delicious, healthy juice.

Ice Crush

For cocktails or slushies, the ICE CRUSH program will be your best helper. The ICE CRUSH setting breaks ice into small pieces for making fine cocktails effortlessly icy or making snow cones in short order.

Chapter 2

Go-To Favorite Recipes

Easy Cheddar Popovers,
page 21

MAKES 2 SERVINGS (ABOUT 3 CUPS)

Hawaiian Pineapple Smoothie

TART **PINEAPPLE** FLAVOR IN A RICH,
IRRESISTIBLE SMOOTHIE.

INGREDIENTS

½ cup pineapple juice

½ cup coconut milk

2 cups fresh pineapple, cut in chunks

1 frozen banana, peeled, cut in half

6 ice cubes

DIRECTIONS

Place ingredients into the blender in the order listed. Press Start and increase the power gradually until the ingredients are well-blended. The smoothie is done when the consistency is smooth and blended to your preference. Divide between glasses and serve.

Calories: 295 Fat: 10g; Chol: 0mg; Sodium: 32mg; Carb: 49g; Fiber: 5g; Protein: 4g

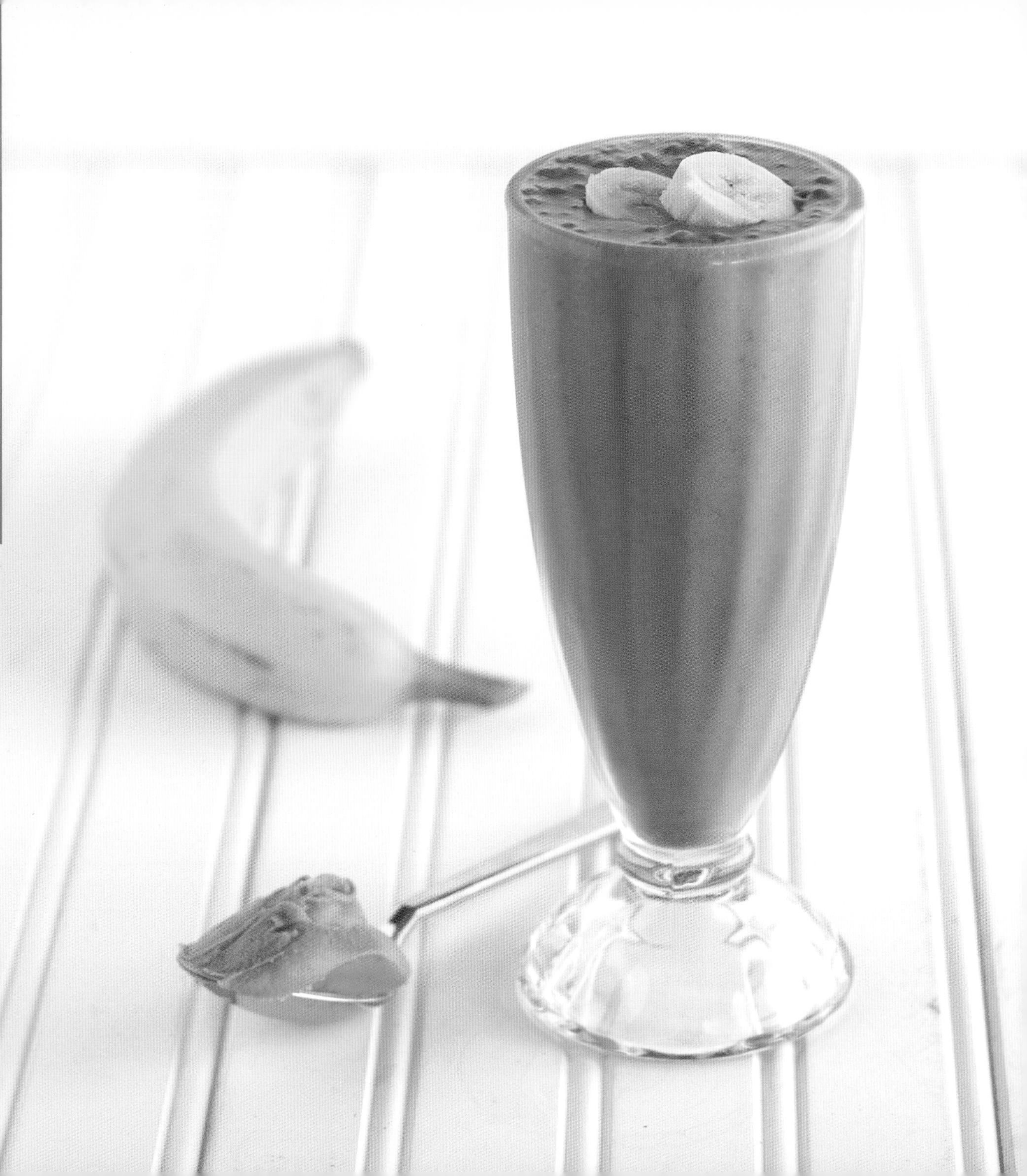

MAKES: 1 SERVING (1¹/₂ CUPS)

PB & C Smoothie

THIS DELICIOUS, **KID-FRIENDLY** SMOOTHIE
MAKES **BREAKFAST** PREP A SNAP.

INGREDIENTS

³/₄ cup chocolate soy milk

1 frozen banana, peeled, cut in half

¹/₄ cup regular or quick-cooking
oats, uncooked (do not use instant
oatmeal)

1 tbsp smooth or creamy peanut
butter

8 ice cubes

DIRECTIONS

Place ingredients into the blender in the order listed. Press Start and
increase the power gradually until the ingredients are well-blended.
The smoothie is done when the consistency is smooth and blended to
your preference. Serve right away.

Calories: 400 Fat: 13g; Chol: 0mg; Sodium: 145mg; Carb: 64g Fiber: 10g Protein: 14g

MAKES 1 SERVING (1¹/₂ CUPS)

Raspberry Morning Smoothie

FRESH **RASPBERRIES** AND ORANGE JUICE OFFER A **SWEET ENERGY BOOST** TO YOUR DAY.

INGREDIENTS

¼ cup orange juice

½ cup fresh raspberries

½ cup vanilla-flavored yogurt

½ tsp chia seeds (optional)

4 frozen Strawberry Orange Starter cubes (see recipe p. 41)

DIRECTIONS

Place ingredients into the blender in the order listed. Press Start and increase the power gradually until the ingredients are well-blended. The smoothie is done when the consistency is smooth and blended to your preference. Serve right away.

Calories: 188 Fat: 3g; Chol: 3mg; Sodium: 87mg; Carb: 40g; Fiber: 4g; Protein: 7g

MAKES ABOUT 1 CUP

Lemony Hollandaise Sauce

A LUSCIOUS **SAUCE** TO COMPLEMENT **EGGS BENEDICT** OR ANY EGG ENTRÉE.

INGREDIENTS

5 large egg yolks

2 tbsp fresh lemon juice

¾ cup + 2 tbsp unsalted butter

pinch cayenne pepper

¼ tsp salt

DIRECTIONS

Press Start and increase power up to the highest speed on the blender. Drop the egg yolks through the lid opening into the blender, one at a time. Add lemon juice and continue blending on high speed to combine. Melt the butter in the microwave oven at 50% power until hot and bubbly. With blender running on medium speed, very slowly add the hot butter, drop by drop at first, through the lid opening. Reduce the speed and continue slowly adding the butter as the sauce thickens. Add the pepper and salt and blend for 10 seconds. Serve at once.

Consuming raw or undercooked meats, poultry, seafood, shellfish, or eggs may increase your risk of foodborne illness.

Calories: 188 Fat: 20g; Chol: 177mg; Sodium: 200mg; Carb: 1g; Fiber: 0g; Protein: 2g

cook's note:

A PERFECT COMPLEMENT TO **lightly steamed** ASPARAGUS OR BROCCOLI, THIS **sauce** IS AT HOME WITH EGGS OR VEGETABLES.

MAKES 4 SERVINGS

Perfect Buttermilk Pancakes

THIS RECIPE COMES TOGETHER SO **QUICKLY**, PANCAKES ARE **HAPPILY** BACK ON THE **WEEKDAY** MENU.

INGREDIENTS

1 cup lowfat buttermilk

1 large egg

2 tbsp canola oil

1 tbsp granulated sugar

¼ tsp pure vanilla extract

pinch salt

1 cup all-purpose white flour

1 tsp baking powder

½ tsp baking soda

DIRECTIONS

Place buttermilk, egg, oil, sugar, vanilla and salt into blender, cover and blend on medium speed until just combined. In a small bowl, combine flour, baking powder and baking soda. With the blender running on medium-low speed, add the flour mixture slowly through the lid opening. Continue blending on medium speed until just combined.

Cook pancakes over medium heat on a nonstick griddle until bubbles form on the surface. Flip pancakes and cook until bottom side is golden. Serve immediately or hold in a warm oven for up to 20 minutes.

Calories: 189 Fat: 4g; Chol: 49mg; Sodium: 250mg; Carb: 30g; Fiber 1g; Protein: 7g

cook's note:

FOR A RICH TREAT, *substitute* BUTTER FOR THE OIL AND ADD **blueberries** TO FINISHED BATTER.

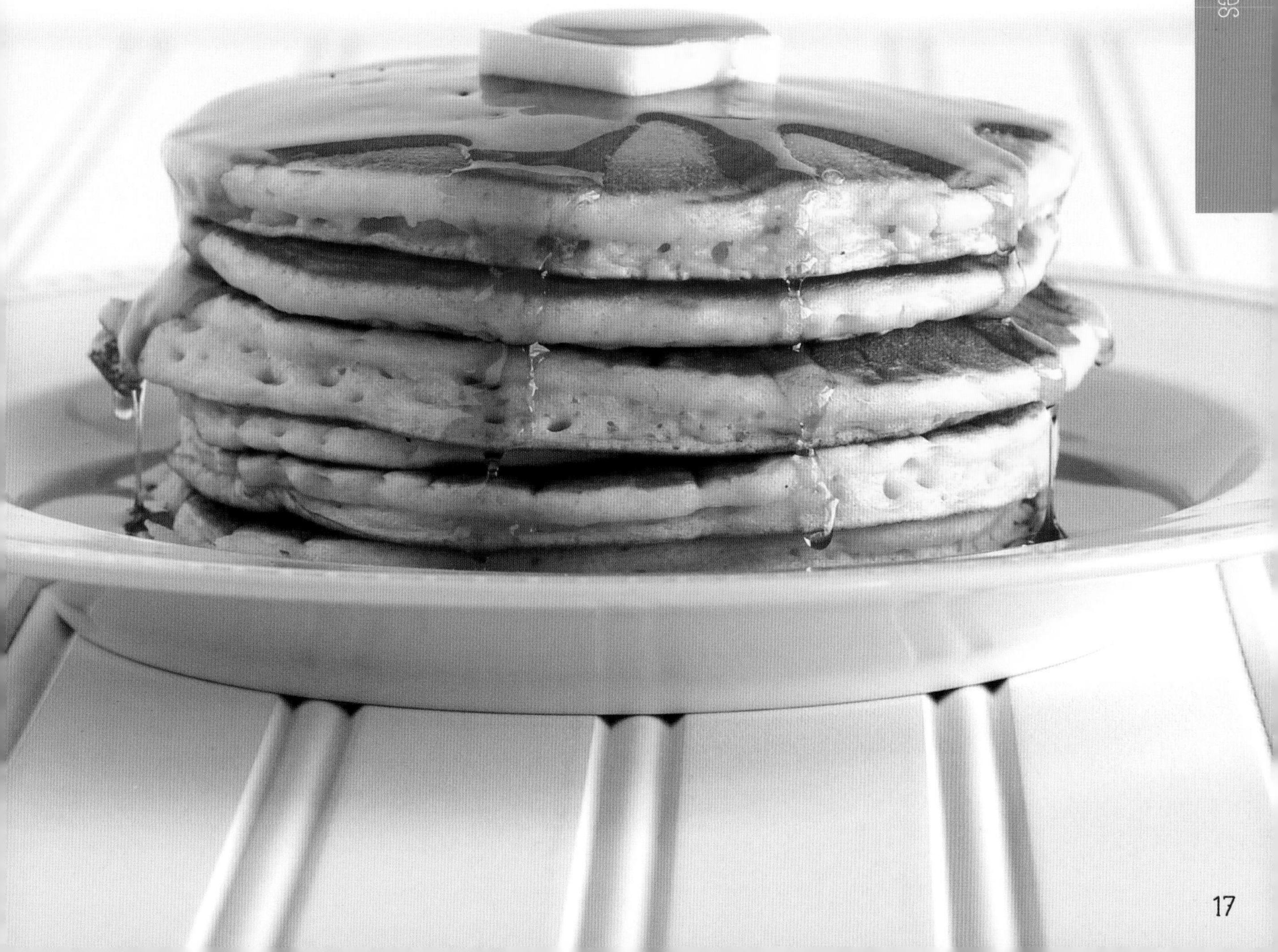

MAKES 3 SERVINGS

Spinach, Sausage and Feta Omelet

BOLD FLAVORS CREATE AN **INVITING OMELET;** GOOD FOR BREAKFAST, A LIGHT LUNCH OR A **SIMPLE DINNER.** BLENDING THE EGGS, BAKING POWDER AND WATER IN THE BLENDER ENSURES A NICE **FLUFFY** OMELET.

INGREDIENTS

3 egg whites

3 large eggs

2 tbsp water

½ tsp baking powder

pinch salt

½ cup feta cheese, crumbled, divided

2 tbsp butter

4 oz. bulk mild Italian sausage, cooked

1 cup baby spinach, loosely packed

DIRECTIONS

Place egg whites, eggs, water, baking powder, salt and 2 tablespoons cheese into the blender and blend on medium speed to combine.

Heat butter in a sauté pan over medium-high heat. Add the egg mixture and reduce heat to medium-low. Cook eggs until just set, about 2 minutes, lifting edges and tipping pan to allow uncooked eggs on top to move into contact with pan. Scatter sausage, spinach and remaining cheese over one half of omelet. Use spatula to flip the other half over the filling. Cook for 10 seconds and slide omelet onto a serving plate. Cut in thirds and serve at once.

Calories: 355 Fat: 28g; Chol: 250mg; Sodium: 658mg; Carb: 4g; Fiber: 1g; Protein: 21g

cook's note:

FRESH HERBS, SUCH AS OREGANO, ADD ANOTHER DELICATE *layer of flavoring* WHEN ADDED TO THE EGGS.

MAKES 18 MUFFINS

Morning Glory Muffins

FINELY CHOPPED **APPLES** AND CARROTS COMBINE WITH **SPICES** TO CREATE QUICK AND **DELICIOUS** MUFFINS.

INGREDIENTS

2 eggs, at room temperature

¾ cup lowfat milk

¼ cup canola oil

½ cup packed brown sugar

1 tsp pure vanilla extract

1 tsp ground cinnamon

1 small apple, peeled, cored, roughly cut

1 small carrot, peeled, roughly cut

1¼ cups all-purpose white flour

1 cup whole wheat flour

1 tsp baking powder

1 tsp baking soda

½ tsp salt

½ cup pineapple, chopped

½ cup golden raisins

½ cup walnuts, chopped

DIRECTIONS

Preheat oven to 350°F. Lightly coat a 12-cup muffin pan and a 6-cup muffin pan with cooking spray or line with paper baking cups. Set aside.

Place eggs, milk, oil, sugar, vanilla, cinnamon, apple and carrot into blender. Pulse on high speed to combine until evenly chopped and chunky-smooth. In a large mixing bowl, combine flours, baking powder, baking soda and salt. Pour the blender mixture into the dry ingredients, stirring just until incorporated. Fold in the pineapple, raisins and walnuts. Spoon batter into prepared muffin cups, filling each about three-fourths full. Bake for 15 to 20 minutes until tops are golden brown and a pick inserted into the center comes out clean. Serve warm.

Calories: 161 Fat: 6g; Chol: 21mg; Sodium: 84mg; Carb: 25g; Fiber: 2g; Protein: 4g

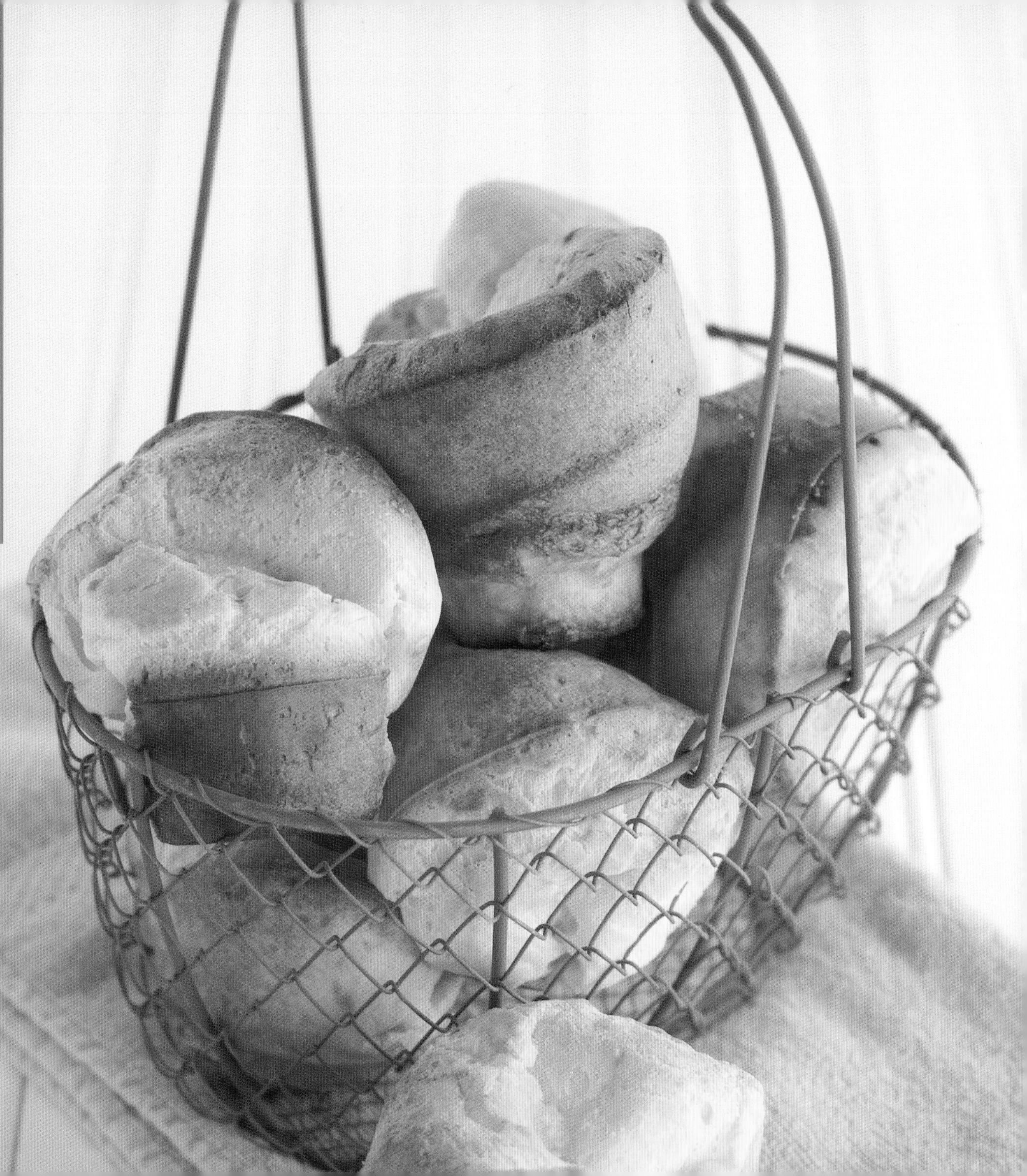

MAKES 12 POPOVERS

Easy Cheddar Popovers

SUPER **EASY** AND ALWAYS IMPRESSIVE, THESE POPOVERS ARE A **GREAT ADDITION** TO A LIGHT **BREAKFAST** OR LUNCHEON. **SPLIT AND SERVE** WITH HONEY OR CHUTNEY.

INGREDIENTS

¼ cup melted butter

2 eggs, at room temperature

1 cup whole milk, room temperature

1 cup all-purpose white flour

½ tsp salt

¼ cup cheddar cheese, roughly chopped

DIRECTIONS

Preheat oven to 400°F. Generously coat a 12-cup muffin pan with melted butter. Set aside.

Place eggs and milk into blender, press Start and blend on medium speed until well-combined. With blender running on medium, slowly add flour and salt through lid opening and blend until just combined. Add cheese and blend on medium speed until smooth. Place muffin pan in oven for a few minutes until butter sizzles. Pour batter into prepared muffin cups. Bake for 28 to 30 minutes, until popovers are puffed and golden. Serve warm.

Calories: 207 Fat: 12g; Chol: 90mg; Sodium: 328mg; Carb: 18g; Fiber: 1g; Protein: 7g

MAKES ABOUT 1³/₄ CUPS

Savory Garlic Hummus

KEEP THE **INGREDIENTS** FOR HUMMUS ON HAND IN YOUR **PANTRY**; IT IS A **PARTY** JUST WAITING FOR AN **OCCASION**. THIS HUMMUS IS A DIP FOR **VEGGIES** AND CHIPS OR SPREAD IT **THICKLY** AS A DELICIOUS SANDWICH SPREAD. FOR A **LIGHT MEAL,** TRY IT ON **HEARTY** SPROUTED WHOLE GRAIN BREAD WITH **ROASTED** VEGETABLES.

INGREDIENTS

15 oz. can garbanzo beans (chickpeas), **liquid drained and reserved**

3 tbsp tahini (sesame seed paste)

2 tbsp lemon juice

3 cloves garlic, roasted

¼ tsp ground cumin

pinch salt

DIRECTIONS

Place all ingredients and 2 tablespoons reserved liquid into the blender. Press Start and increase the power gradually to medium speed. Blend until the spread is well-blended and smooth. Add more liquid, if needed, to reach desired consistency.

Calories: 109 Fat: 4g; Chol: 0mg; Sodium: 138mg; Carb: 14g; Fiber: 4g; Protein: 5g

- To roast garlic, slice one-fourth inch off the pointed end of a head of garlic. Place garlic head on a square of foil and drizzle with olive oil. Add herbs, if desired, loosely wrap and place in a 350°F oven for about 40 minutes, or until garlic has softened. Cool slightly and use fingers to pop cloves from their papery skins. Use as desired.

cook's note:

ROASTED *garlic* IS SLIGHTLY SWEET AND *smoky-flavored*.

MAKES 6 TO 8 SERVINGS

Roasted Tomato Salsa Guacamole

EVERYBODY'S **FAVORITE** WHIPS TOGETHER IN A **SNAP**.
SERVE WITH WHITE AND BLUE **CORN CHIPS** FOR A
FESTIVE PRESENTATION.

INGREDIENTS

3 large ripe avocados, peeled and pitted

1 large lime, juiced

3 tbsp roasted tomato salsa

½ tsp salt

DIRECTIONS

Place avocados, lime juice, salsa and salt into the blender and Pulse to desired consistency. Scrape down the sides of the blender as needed. Taste and adjust seasonings. Serve immediately or cover and chill.

Calories: 124 Fat: 11g; Chol: 0mg; Sodium: 157mg; Carb: 7g; Fiber: 5g; Protein: 2g

cook's note:

FOR A **spicy** GUACAMOLE, ADD ONE-HALF **jalapeño** PEPPER WITH SEEDS BEFORE BLENDING.

MAKES ABOUT 2¹/₂ CUPS

Homemade French Onion Dip

A **FRIENDLY** AND FABULOUS HOMEMADE DIP FOR YOUR NEXT GATHERING. CUCUMBERS, **CARROTS**, CELERY AND **RED PEPPER STRIPS** ARE COLORFUL ADDITIONS TO SERVE ALONGSIDE.

INGREDIENTS

3 tbsp canola oil

2 yellow onions, peeled and thinly sliced

1 cup sour cream

8 oz cream cheese, room temperature

½ tsp Worcestershire sauce

½ tsp garlic powder

½ tsp salt

DIRECTIONS

Heat oil over medium-high heat, add onions and sauté for 5 minutes, stirring frequently to avoid burning. Reduce heat and cook, stirring occasionally, until onions are softened and nicely browned, about 25 minutes. Set aside and cool. Reserve 2 tablespoons for garnish.

Place remaining onions in blender and add remaining ingredients. Press Start and gradually increase the speed to high. Blend until the mixture is mostly smooth. Transfer to a serving bowl, cover tightly and chill for at least 1 hour. Garnish with reserved caramelized onions and serve.

Calories: 204 Fat: 19g; Chol: 44mg; Sodium: 249mg; Carb: 5g; Fiber: 1g; Protein: 3g

cook's note:

SAVE TIME! **Double** THE RECIPE FOR **caramelized** ONIONS. FREEZE UNTIL USE.

MAKES 4 SERVINGS

Broccoli & White Cheddar Soup in Sourdough Bowls

SMOOTH, DELICIOUS AND **COMFORTING**. THIS SOUP WILL MAKE A LASTING **IMPRESSION**.

INGREDIENTS

2 tbsp olive oil

½ yellow onion, peeled and chopped

1 clove garlic, finely chopped

1 lb broccoli, trimmed and cut into florets

¼ cup basil leaves

3 cups vegetable broth

salt and ground black pepper to taste

1½ cups Dubliner cheese, shredded (or use any shredded cheddar cheese)

1 tsp salt

1 tsp ground black pepper

4 small sourdough bread rounds

DIRECTIONS

Heat a deep sauté pan over medium heat and add oil when heated. Sauté onion until softened, stirring frequently. Add garlic and sauté for one minute. Increase heat to high and add broccoli, basil, vegetable broth, salt and pepper. Reduce heat and simmer until broccoli is tender, about 6 minutes. Carefully transfer mixture to blender and add the cheese, salt and pepper. Press Start and blend on medium speed until smooth and well-blended. Taste and adjust seasonings.

Trim the top from each of the bread rounds and remove the inner bread, leaving a one-half inch thick bowl. Ladle soup into sourdough bowls and serve while hot.

Calories: 585 Fat: 23g; Chol: 45mg; Sodium: 2146mg; Carb: 71g; Fiber: 5g; Protein: 25g

MAKES 8 TO 10 SERVINGS

Winter Minestrone Soup

HEARTY INGREDIENTS COMBINE TO MAKE A **SUBSTANTIAL**, FLAVORFUL SOUP.

INGREDIENTS

2 tbsp olive oil

1 onion, peeled and chopped

2 carrots, peeled and chopped

2 ribs celery, cut into large pieces

2 cloves garlic, minced

28 oz can whole tomatoes, with juice

4 cups chicken or vegetable stock

1 russet potato, peeled and cubed

1 tsp dried oregano

1 bay leaf

½ tsp salt

1 tsp freshly ground black pepper

½ head green cabbage, cored and shredded

1 yellow squash, thickly sliced

15 oz can garbanzo beans (chickpeas), drained and rinsed

1 cup small pasta (shells, elbows, etc.), uncooked

freshly grated Parmesan cheese for garnish

chopped fresh basil for garnish

DIRECTIONS

In a large stockpot, heat oil over medium heat. Add onion, carrots and celery and sauté until softened. Add garlic and sauté for 1 minute. Add tomatoes with juice, chicken stock, potato, oregano, bay leaf, salt and pepper and bring to a boil. Partially cover, lower heat and simmer until potatoes are tender, about 10 minutes. Remove bay leaf and carefully transfer one-half of the soup into the blender (no more than 6 cups). Cover and Pulse on medium speed until soup is smooth. Return mixture to stockpot. Add cabbage, squash, beans and pasta and simmer for 15 to 20 minutes, until vegetables are tender and pasta is cooked al dente. Adjust seasonings and serve hot, garnished with Parmesan cheese and basil.

Calories: 173 Fat: 2g; Chol: 3mg; Sodium: 709mg; Carb: 16g; Fiber: 7g; Protein: 8g

MAKES 2 SERVINGS

Chinese Chicken Salad with Sesame Ginger Vinaigrette

ALTHOUGH YOU CAN OFTEN FIND THIS SALAD ON A **MENU**, IT IS TYPICALLY **HEAVILY DOUSED** WITH A SWEETISH **ASIAN SAUCE**, WHICH CAN OVERWHELM THE SALAD. THIS ALTERNATIVE INTRODUCES A LIGHTER DRESSING WITH ORGANIC **HONEY** INSTEAD OF SUGAR.

INGREDIENTS

Salad

3 cups romaine lettuce, chopped

1 cup Napa cabbage, chopped

1 cup red cabbage, chopped

1 carrot, peeled and shredded

6 oz chicken breast, grilled, cooled and thinly sliced

2 green onions, trimmed and chopped

¼ cup roasted cashews

¼ cup crispy chow mein noodles

Vinaigrette

2 tbsp canola oil

2 tbsp rice wine vinegar

1 tsp soy sauce

1 tsp Dijon mustard

¼ tsp sesame oil

¼-inch piece fresh ginger root, peeled

2 tbsp organic honey

1 tsp sesame seeds

DIRECTIONS

Place canola oil, vinegar, soy sauce, mustard, sesame oil, ginger and honey into the blender. Press Start and blend on a medium-high speed until smooth. Add sesame seeds and Pulse to combine. Set aside.

In a large serving bowl, toss lettuce, cabbages and carrot. Add one-fourth cup vinaigrette and toss to coat. Divide salad mixture between plates and top with chicken breast, green onions, cashews and crispy noodles. Drizzle with additional vinaigrette before serving.

Calories: 466 Fat: 21g; Chol: 52g; Sodium: 330mg; Carb: 33g; Fiber: 4g; Protein: 27g

MAKES 6 SERVINGS

Vegan Broccoli Sunflower Slaw

THIS **CRUNCHY** SIDE DISH WILL **GET RAVE REVIEWS** FROM YOUR GUESTS, VEGANS AND **CARNIVORES** ALIKE.

INGREDIENTS

4 cups broccoli florets

1 lemon

½ cup vegan mayonnaise

2 tbsp raspberry vinegar

½ tsp salt

1 tsp ground black pepper

½ cup dried cranberries

½ cup sunflower seeds, roasted

½ cup almonds, chopped

DIRECTIONS

Place florets into blender, add water to cover and Pulse until chopped. Drain water and transfer broccoli to large mixing bowl. Zest the lemon and juice it. Place zest, juice, mayonnaise, raspberry vinegar, salt and pepper into blender. Press Start and gradually increase the power to medium. Blend for 30 seconds. Pour dressing over broccoli, add remaining ingredients and toss to combine. Cover and refrigerate for at least two hours. Serve chilled.

Calories: 21 Fat: 14g; Chol: 0mg; Sodium: 279mg; Carb: 20g; Fiber: 5g; Protein: 6g

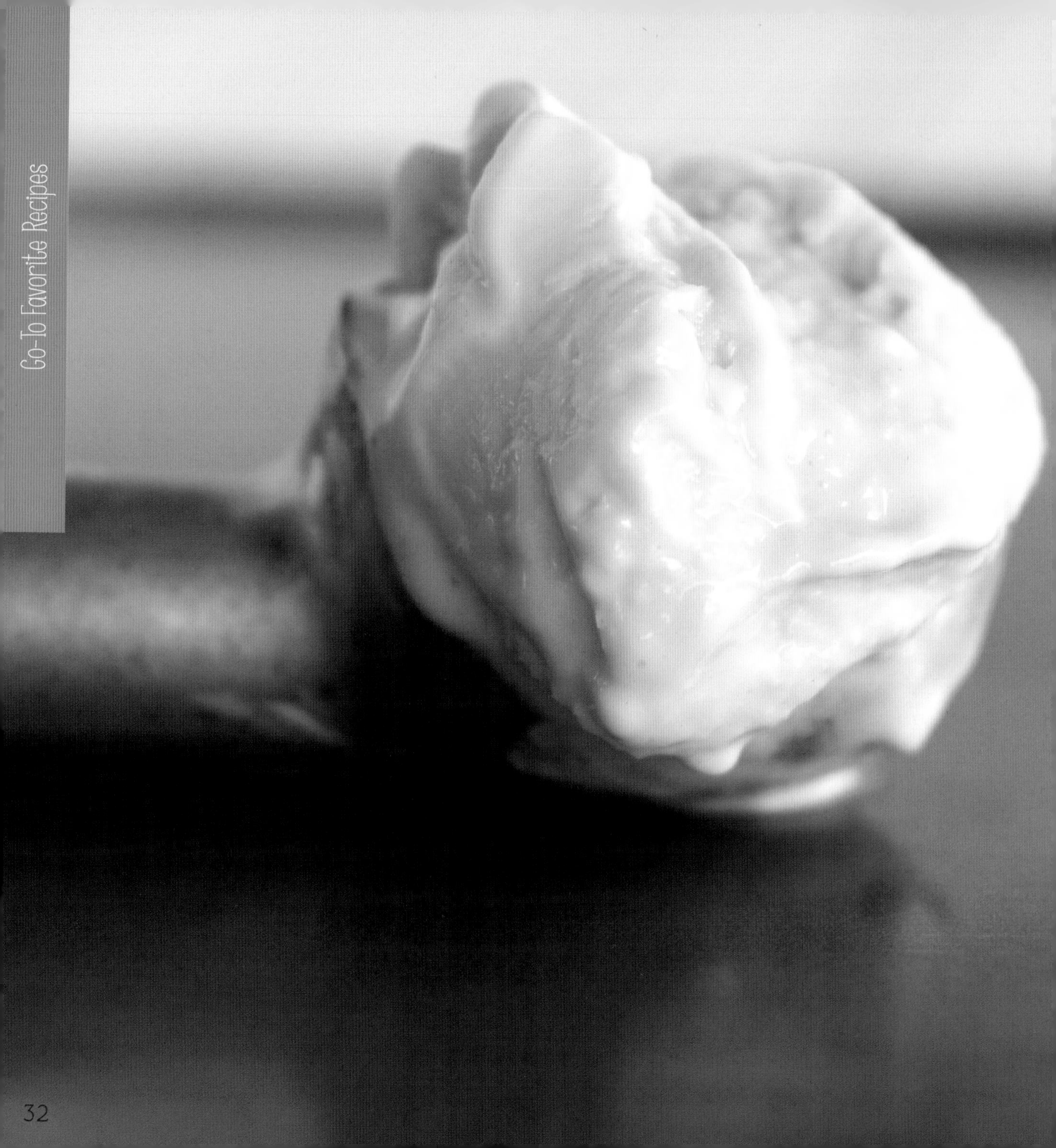

MAKES 3 TO 4 SERVINGS

Triple Treat Freeze

TART AND SWEET WITH A **HINT OF VANILLA,** THIS DELECTABLE FROZEN DESSERT WHIPS UP IN MINUTES AND FREEZES IN A **COUPLE OF HOURS** WITHOUT THE USE OF AN **ICE CREAM MAKER.** USE AS A **SWEET** STAND-IN FOR WHIPPED CREAM WHEN PREPARING STRAWBERRY SHORTCAKE OR SERVE IT WITH ANY **FRESH FRUIT** IN DESSERT BOWLS.

INGREDIENTS

1½ cups plain kefir

6 tbsp sweetened condensed milk

1½ tsp pure vanilla extract

pinch salt

DIRECTIONS

Place all ingredients in blender and press Start. Pulse until the mixture is very smooth. Pour into a shallow 2-quart pan, cover and place in freezer. Using the tines of a fork, stir the mixture every 30 to 40 minutes for at least 2 hours until well-frozen, creating an icy texture. Scoop and serve while frozen.

Calories: 162 Fat: 5g; Chol: 19mg; Sodium: 83mg; Carb: 22g; Fiber: 0g; Protein: 6g

MAKES 6 TO 8 TO 10 SERVINGS

Blue Ribbon Mac & Cheese

THE **BEST** MAC N'CHEESE ON THE PLANET
STARTS IN A **BLENDER**; WHO KNEW?

INGREDIENTS

2 cups Blender White Sauce
(see page 189)

¼ tsp ground nutmeg

½ tsp kosher salt

½ tsp ground black pepper

4 cups white cheddar cheese,
shredded (or use any shredded
cheddar cheese)

2 cups gruyere cheese, shredded

16 oz pkg small penne pasta,
cooked and drained

1 cup plain panko crumbs

DIRECTIONS

Make sauce as directed. Whisk in nutmeg, salt and pepper.

Preheat the oven to 350°F. Coat a Dutch oven or deep 3-quart casserole
dish with cooking spray. Combine the Blender White Sauce, cheddar
and gruyere cheeses in the dish and add the penne pasta. Mix again until
combined. Top with panko crumbs. Bake for 45 minutes, or until cheeses
are melted and top is crusty and golden brown. Let stand for 5 minutes
before serving.

Calories: 537 Fat: 28g; Chol: 75mg; Sodium: 655mg; Carb: 44g; Fiber: 2g; Protein: 26g

Chapter 3

Smoothies, Smoothies & More Smoothies

Super Simple
Strawberry Goodness,
page 43

MAKES 2 SERVINGS (3 CUPS)

Peach, Mango & Honey Smoothie

RIPE, **PEAK–FLAVOR FRUIT** MAKES THIS SMOOTHIE ESPECIALLY **INVITING**. LOOK FOR IN-SEASON **ORGANIC** FRUIT AT YOUR LOCAL MARKET.

INGREDIENTS

2 fresh peaches, peeled and pitted

1½ cups frozen mango, cut in chunks

1 lemon, peeled, cut in half, seeded

1 cup water

1 tbsp honey

6 ice cubes

DIRECTIONS

Place ingredients into the blender in the order listed. Press Start and increase the power gradually until the ingredients are well-blended. The smoothie is done when the consistency is smooth and blended to your preference. Divide between glasses and serve.

Calories: 201 Fat: 1g; Chol: 0mg; Sodium: 2mg; Carb: 52g; Fiber: 6g; Protein: 3g

MAKES 2 SERVINGS (ABOUT 3 CUPS)

Berry Peachy Smoothie

PACKED WITH FRUIT, THIS IS A **SWEETLY FILLING** SMOOTHIE!

INGREDIENTS

½ cup fresh strawberries

2 ripe peaches, peeled, pitted, cut in half

6 oz peach-flavored Greek yogurt

1 frozen banana, peeled, cut in half

4 frozen Strawberry Orange Starter cubes (see recipe p. 41)

DIRECTIONS

Place ingredients into the blender in the order listed. Press Start and increase the power gradually until the ingredients are well-blended. The smoothie is done when the consistency is smooth and blended to your preference. Divide between glasses and serve..

Calories: 225 Fat: 1g; Chol: 2mg; Sodium: 44mg; Carb: 54g; Fiber: 7g; Protein: 7g

cook's note:

FREEZE *overripe* BANANAS FOR USE IN YOUR MORNING *smoothie*.

MAKES: 2 SERVINGS

Carrot Orange Dream

INVITING **CARROT** AND FRUIT BLENDS UP WITH COOL **PEACH YOGURT**. SUBSTITUTE OTHER FLAVORED YOGURT **VARIETIES** AS DESIRED.

INGREDIENTS

½ cup orange juice

6 oz peach-flavored Greek yogurt

1 large carrot, peeled and quartered

1 frozen banana, peeled, cut in half

½ cup frozen mango, cut in chunks

8 ice cubes

DIRECTIONS

Place ingredients into the blender in the order listed. Press Start and increase the power gradually until the ingredients are well-blended. The smoothie is done when the consistency is smooth and blended to your preference. Divide between glasses and serve.

Calories: 218 Fat: 3g; Chol: 9mg; Sodium: 55mg; Carb: 43g; Fiber: 4g; Protein: 9g

MAKES 3–4 SERVINGS (4 CUPS)

Pom Punch Smoothie

THIS SMOOTHIE **PACKS** A PUNCH OF **BRIGHT** FLAVOR!

INGREDIENTS

¾ **cup pomegranate juice**

¼ **cup apple juice**

1½ **cups pineapple, cut in chunks**

1½ **cups frozen strawberries**

1 **cup frozen mango, cut in chunks**

6 **ice cubes**

DIRECTIONS

Place ingredients into the blender in the order listed. Press Start and increase the power gradually until the ingredients are well-blended. The smoothie is done when the consistency is smooth and blended to your preference. Divide between glasses and serve.

Calories: 110 Fat 1g; Chol: 0mg; Sodium: 2mg; Carb: 28g; Fiber: 3g; Protein: 2g

MAKES 10 TO 12 CUBES

Strawberry Orange Starter

A **CONDENSED** JUICE, FROZEN INTO CUBES,
SWEETENS YOUR GREEN SMOOTHIES IN A **SNAP**
AND ADDS FROZEN **TANG** TO ANY FRUIT SMOOTHIE.

INGREDIENTS

¼ cup orange juice

1 cup strawberries, hulled

1 navel orange, peeled and pith removed

DIRECTIONS

Place ingredients into the blender in the order listed. Press Start and increase the power gradually until the ingredients are well-blended and smooth. Pour the starter into an ice cube tray and freeze until solid. Transfer cubes to a self-sealing plastic bag and store in freezer until needed.

Calories: 12 Fat: 0g; Chol: 0mg; Sodium: 0mg; Carb: 3g; Fiber: 1g; Protein: 0g

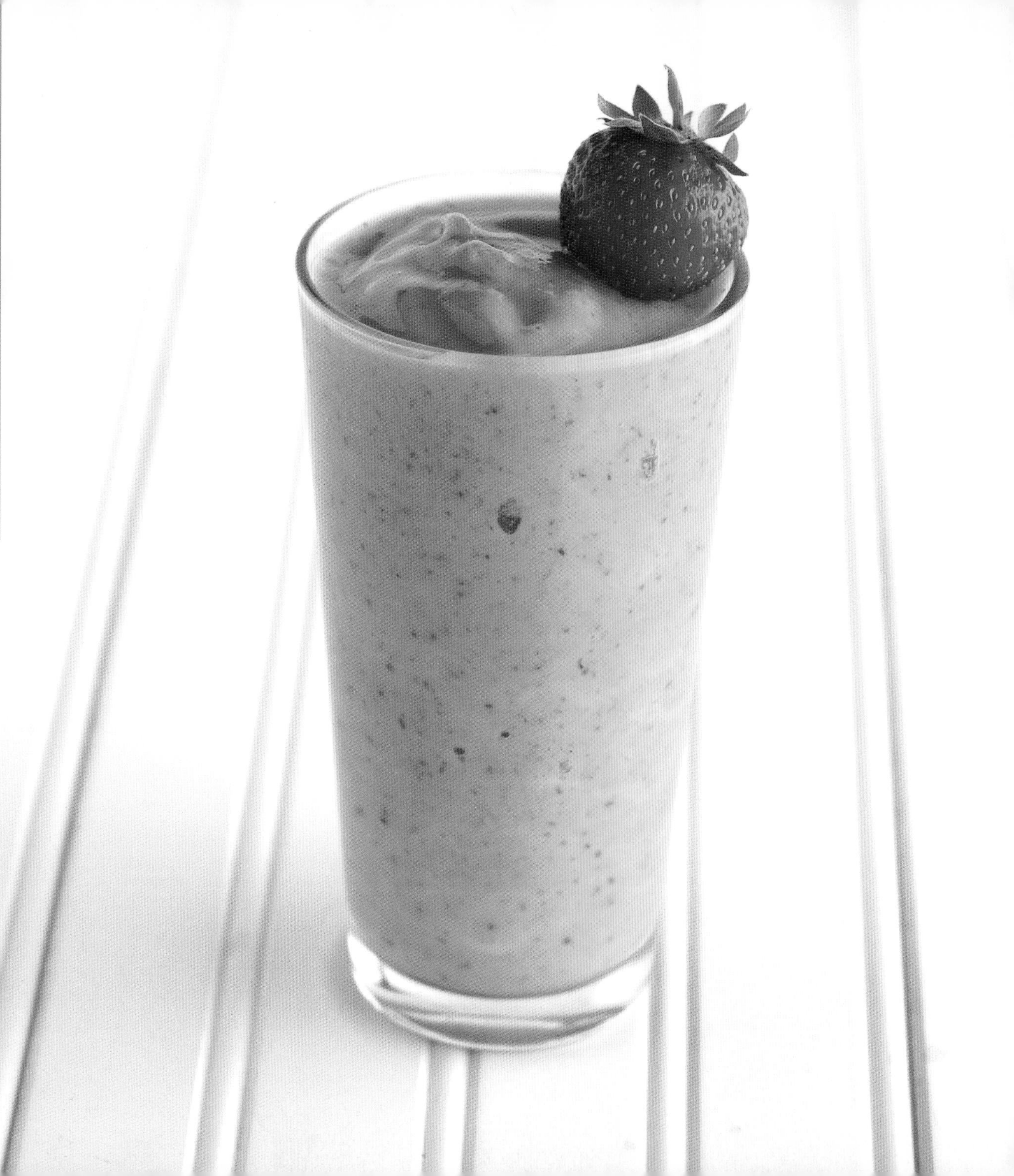

MAKES 1–2 SERVINGS (ABOUT 2¹/₂ CUPS)

Super Simple Strawberry Goodness

AN **EASY-TO-PREP** SMOOTHIE THAT WILL **CARRY YOU** THROUGH EVERY DAY OF THE **WEEK**.

INGREDIENTS

1 cup lowfat vanilla yogurt

1 large banana, peeled, cut in half

1½ cups frozen strawberries

6 ice cubes

DIRECTIONS

Place ingredients into the blender in the order listed. Press Start and increase the power gradually until the ingredients are well-blended. The smoothie is done when the consistency is smooth and blended to your preference. Divide between glasses and serve.

Calories: 177 Fat: 2g; Chol: 2mg; Sodium: 87mg; Carb: 38g; Fiber: 5g; Protein: 8g

MAKES 2 TO 3 SERVINGS (ABOUT 3¼ CUPS)

Duo Peach Sweetness

NATURE'S OWN **SWEET**, RIPE PEACHES AND
NECTAR MAKE THIS A **SUMMER** DESSERT-IN-A-GLASS.

INGREDIENTS

1 cup peach nectar, chilled

2 large ripe peaches, peeled and pitted

8 ice cubes

DIRECTIONS

Place ingredients into the blender in the order listed. Press Start and increase the power gradually until the ingredients are well-blended. The smoothie is done when the consistency is smooth and blended to your preference. Divide between glasses and serve.

Calories: 103 Fat: 0g; Chol: 0mg; Sodium: 6mg; Carb: 27g; Fiber: 3g; Protein: 2g

cook's note:

IF USING *frozen* PEACHES, SUBSTITUTE 6 *ice cubes* AND 1 CUP NECTAR.

MAKES 2 SERVINGS (ABOUT 2 CUPS)

Chocolate-Covered Strawberry Smoothie

ADD A **SWIRL** OF CHOCOLATE **HAZELNUT SPREAD** ON TOP OF THIS BLENDED SMOOTHIE AS A RICH GARNISH.

INGREDIENTS

½ cup lowfat milk

1½ cups fresh strawberries, hulled

2 tbsp chocolate hazelnut spread

8 ice cubes

DIRECTIONS

Place ingredients into the blender in the order listed. Press Start and increase the power gradually until the ingredients are well-blended. The smoothie is done when the consistency is smooth and blended to your preference. Divide between glasses and serve.

Calories: 163 Fat 7g; Chol: 3mg; Sodium: 41mg; Carb: 23g; Fiber: 3g; Protein: 4g

MAKES 2 TO 3 SERVINGS (ABOUT 3 CUPS)

Strawberries n' Cream Smoothie

LUSCIOUSLY **WHIPPED** INTO SWEETNESS!

INGREDIENTS

1 cup lowfat milk

2 cups frozen strawberries

½ cup vanilla-flavored Greek yogurt

1 to 2 tbsp sugar (as desired)

½ tsp almond extract (optional)

DIRECTIONS

Place ingredients into the blender in the order listed. Press Start and increase the power gradually until the ingredients are well-blended. The smoothie is done when the consistency is smooth and blended to your preference. Divide between glasses and serve.

Calories: 114 Fat 3g; Chol: 8mg; Sodium: 56mg; Carb: 17g; Fiber: 2g; Protein: 7g

MAKES 1 SERVING (ABOUT 1¹/₄ CUPS)

Peanut Butter & Jelly Smoothie

A DELECTABLE **AFTERNOON SNACK** IN A GLASS.

INGREDIENTS

1 cup vanilla almond milk

³/₄ cup frozen blueberries

¹/₂ cup frozen raspberries

1 tbsp creamy or chunky peanut butter

DIRECTIONS

Place ingredients into the blender in the order listed. Press Start and increase the power gradually until the ingredients are well-blended. The smoothie is done when the consistency is smooth and blended to your preference. Serve right away.

Calories: 249 Fat 11g; Chol: 0mg; Sodium: 225mg; Carb: 34g; Fiber: 9g; Protein: 7g

MAKES 3 TO 4 SERVINGS (ABOUT 4 CUPS)

Sunrise Smoothie

USE **FRESH** OR **FROZEN** FRUIT IN THIS DELIGHTFUL SMOOTHIE. ADD ORANGE JUICE, IF NEEDED, TO **THIN THE MIXTURE** WHILE BLENDING.

INGREDIENTS

1 cup fresh strawberries, hulled

1 cup fresh peaches, peeled and pitted

1 cup frozen mango, cut in chunks

6 ice cubes

DIRECTIONS

Place ingredients into the blender in the order listed. Press Start and increase the power gradually until the ingredients are well-blended. The smoothie is done when the consistency is smooth and blended to your preference. Divide between glasses and serve.

Calories: 67 Fat: 1g; Chol: 0mg; Sodium: 1mg; Carb: 17g; Fiber: 3g; Protein: 1g

MAKES 2 SERVINGS (2½ CUPS)

Pineapple, Kale & Kiwi Smoothie

THIS SWEET AND CREAMY SMOOTHIE WILL **FOOL** EVEN
THE **SAVVIEST** GREENS-RESISTER.

INGREDIENTS

¾ cup water

1 cup fresh pineapple, cut in chunks

4 large leaves kale

2 kiwi fruit, peeled

½ Granny Smith apple, cored

½ cup green grapes

8 ice cubes

DIRECTIONS

Place ingredients into the blender in the order listed. Press Start and increase the power gradually until the ingredients are well-blended. The smoothie is done when the consistency is smooth and blended to your preference. Divide between glasses and serve.

Calories: 111 Fat 1g; Chol: 1mg; Sodium: 9mg; Carb: 20g; Fiber: 4g; Protein: 3g

cook's note:

SUBSTITUTE
SWISS CHARD OR
baby spinach leaves
FOR THE KALE.

49

MAKES 2 SERVINGS (ABOUT 3 CUPS)

Cucumber, Kiwi, Celery & Apple Smoothie

CUCUMBER AND KIWI FRUIT ARE ESPECIALLY **DELICATE** IN FLAVOR. THE **TART APPLE** BRINGS A SNAP OF **BRIGHT FLAVOR**.

INGREDIENTS

1 cup water

1 cucumber, peeled, cut in large pieces

2 kiwi fruit, peeled

2 ribs celery, cut into large pieces

1 Granny Smith apple, peeled, cored and cut in chunks

4 ice cubes

DIRECTIONS

Place ingredients into the blender in the order listed. Press Start and increase the power gradually until the ingredients are well-blended. The smoothie is done when the consistency is smooth and blended to your preference. Divide between glasses and serve.

Calories: 104 Fat: 1g; Chol: 0mg; Sodium: 19mg; Carb: 25g; Fiber: 5g; Protein: 2g

MAKES 1 SERVING (ABOUT 1¹/₃ CUPS)

Pomegranate Jeweled Smoothie

WHEN **POMEGRANATES** ARE IN SEASON, TOSS IN A HANDFUL OF **SEEDS** TO **BOOST** THE FLAVOR OF THIS **JEWELED** SMOOTHIE.

INGREDIENTS

½ cup pomegranate juice

½ cucumber, peeled and halved

4 leaves hearts of romaine lettuce

½ cup frozen pineapple, cut in chunks

¼-inch fresh ginger root, peeled

1 tsp cilantro leaves (optional)

3 ice cubes

DIRECTIONS

Place ingredients into the blender in the order listed. Press Start and increase the power gradually until the ingredients are well-blended. The smoothie is done when the consistency is smooth and blended to your preference. Serve at once.

Calories: 128 Fat 0g; Chol: 0mg; Sodium: 4mg; Carb: 33g; Fiber: 3g; Protein: 1g

MAKES 2 SERVINGS (ABOUT 2½ CUPS)

Strawberry, Grape & Banana Smoothie

THERE IS NO BETTER WAY TO **START YOUR DAY!**

CHOOSE SEASONAL RIPE, ORGANIC BERRIES AND GRAPES.

SUBSTITUTE **SOY MILK** OR LOWFAT MILK, AS DESIRED.

INGREDIENTS

1 cup almond milk

½ cup seedless red grapes

1 large frozen banana, peeled, cut in half

6 large frozen strawberries

1 tsp green plant protein powder (use any protein powder, if desired)

6 ice cubes

DIRECTIONS

Place ingredients into the blender in the order listed. Press Start and increase the power gradually until the ingredients are well-blended. The smoothie is done when the consistency is smooth and blended to your preference. Divide between glasses and serve.

Calories: 143 Fat 2g; Chol: 10mg; Sodium: 88mg; Carb: 30g; Fiber: 4g; Protein: 6g

MAKES 2 SERVINGS (ABOUT 2½ CUPS)

Chocolate, Peanut Butter & Banana Smoothie

THE **CLASSIC** FLAVOR COMBINATION OF **CHOCOLATE** AND PEANUT BUTTER CREATE AN ENTICING SMOOTHIE.

INGREDIENTS

1½ cups unsweetened hemp milk (use lowfat milk, if desired)

2 tbsp cocoa powder

2 tbsp creamy or chunky peanut butter

2 large frozen bananas, peeled, cut in half

DIRECTIONS

Place ingredients into the blender in the order listed. Press Start and increase the power gradually until the ingredients are well-blended. The smoothie is done when the consistency is smooth and blended to your preference. Divide between glasses and serve.

Calories: 276 Fat: 15g; Chol: 0mg; Sodium: 76mg; Carb: 37g; Fiber: 7g; Protein: 7g

MAKES 2 SERVINGS (ABOUT 3 CUPS)

Breakfast Big Berry Blast Smoothie

GO **BIG** ON BERRIES IN THIS **SPECTACULAR** SMOOTHIE!

INGREDIENTS

½ cup pure cranberry juice

¾ cup water

2 scoops breakfast protein powder

½ cup nonfat vanilla yogurt

1 cup frozen mixed berries

4 ice cubes

DIRECTIONS

Place ingredients into the blender in the order listed. Press Start and increase the power gradually until the ingredients are well-blended. The smoothie is done when the consistency is smooth and blended to your preference. Divide between glasses and serve.

Calories: 210 Fat: 3g; Chol: 62mg; Sodium: 122mg; Carb: 28g; Fiber: 3g; Protein: 21g

MAKES 2 SERVINGS (ABOUT 2¹/₂ CUPS)

Tangerine Dream Smoothie

FLAVORFULLY **SWEET** AND **BEAUTIFUL**!

INGREDIENTS

1 cup almond milk (use lowfat, if desired)

2 large tangerines or mandarin oranges, peeled

¹/₄ cup regular or quick-cooking oats, uncooked (do not use instant oatmeal)

¹/₂ cup frozen blueberries

1 frozen banana, peeled, cut in half

8 ice cubes

DIRECTIONS

Place ingredients into the blender in the order listed. Press Start and increase the power gradually until the ingredients are well-blended. The smoothie is done when the consistency is smooth and blended to your preference. Divide between glasses and serve.

Calories: 200 Fat: 3g; Chol: 0mg; Sodium: 78mg; Carb: 44g; Fiber: 6g; Protein: 4g

MAKES 1 SERVING (ABOUT 1¹/₂ CUPS)

Zeus Boost Smoothie

THE **GREEK GODS** PROBABLY FEASTED ON **SMOOTHIES** SUCH AS THIS.

INGREDIENTS

¹/₃ cup unsweetened vanilla almond milk

1 cup nonfat plain Greek yogurt

3 large strawberries, hulled

2 tsp honey

¹/₂ cup frozen blueberries

6 ice cubes

DIRECTIONS

Place ingredients into the blender in the order listed. Press Start and increase the power gradually until the ingredients are well-blended. The smoothie is done when the consistency is smooth and blended to your preference. Serve right away.

Calories: 246 Fat 1g; Chol: 15mg; Sodium: 122mg; Carb: 39g; Fiber: 1g; Protein: 23g

MAKES 1 TO 2 SERVINGS (ABOUT 2 CUPS)

Oats n' Apple Pie Smoothie

APPLE PIE FOR **BREAKFAST**! THE COMBINED YOGURT, OATS AND FRUIT CREATE A SMOOTHIE THAT **TASTES** JUST LIKE YOUR **GRANDMOTHER'S APPLE PIE**. WITH ALL THE **DELICIOUSNESS** PACKED INSIDE, YOU'LL BE **POWERED-UP** FOR THE DAY!

INGREDIENTS

1 cup lowfat vanilla yogurt

3 tbsp unsweetened vanilla almond milk

1 Granny Smith apple, cored, peeled and quartered

¼ cup regular or quick-cooking oats, uncooked (do not use instant oatmeal)

2 tbsp maple syrup

¼ tsp pure vanilla extract

dash ground cinnamon

10 ice cubes

DIRECTIONS

Place ingredients into the blender in the order listed. Press Start and increase the power gradually until the ingredients are well-blended. The smoothie is done when the consistency is smooth and blended to your preference. Serve right away.

Calories: 237 Fat 1g; Chol: 85mg; Sodium: 93mg; Carb: 48g; Fiber: 4g; Protein: 8g

MAKES: 2 SERVINGS

Cha-Cha Chocolate Smoothie

NO ONE WILL GUESS THERE IS **SPINACH** IN THIS **CHOCOLATE LOVER'S** SMOOTHIE.

INGREDIENTS

½ cup unsweetened chocolate almond milk

½ cup baby spinach, loosely packed

1 tbsp chocolate hazelnut spread

1 tbsp dark cocoa powder

1 banana, peeled, cut in half

8-10 ice cubes

DIRECTIONS

Place ingredients into the blender in the order listed. Press Start and increase the power gradually until the ingredients are well-blended. The smoothie is done when the consistency is smooth and blended to your preference. Divide between glasses and serve.

Calories: 141 Fat: 4g; Chol: 0mg; Sodium: 49mg; Carb: 25g; Fiber: 4g; Protein: 3g

cook's note:

A PERFECT WAY TO **add** VEGGIES TO YOUR **child's** DAY!

 **MAKES 2 SERVINGS (ABOUT 3 CUPS)**

Nutty Pumpkin Pecan Smoothie

IMAGINE COMBINING A **PUMPKIN PIE** WITH A **PECAN PIE...** BUT WITHOUT ALL THE **FUSSY** BAKING.

TRY IT WITH A DOLLOP OF WHIPPED CREAM!

INGREDIENTS

1 cup lowfat milk

2 tbsp maple syrup

6 oz lowfat vanilla yogurt

1 cup canned or fresh pumpkin purée

¼ teaspoon ground pumpkin pie spice

pinch ground cinnamon

¼ cup pecans, toasted

12 ice cubes

DIRECTIONS

Place ingredients into the blender in the order listed. Press Start and increase the power gradually until the ingredients are well-blended. The smoothie is done when the consistency is smooth and blended to your preference. Divide between glasses and serve.

Calories: 399 Fat: 12g; Chol: 7mg; Sodium: 411mg; Carb: 67g; Fiber: 13g; Protein: 12g

MAKES 2 TO 3 SERVINGS (ABOUT 3 CUPS)

Watermelon & Double Berry Smoothie

DELIGHTFULLY, **NATURALLY** REFRESHING.

INGREDIENTS

½ cup cherry juice

2 tbsp honey

½ cup seedless watermelon, cut in chunks

½ cup frozen strawberries

½ cup frozen raspberries

DIRECTIONS

Place ingredients into the blender in the order listed. Press Start and increase the power gradually until the ingredients are well-blended. The smoothie is done when the consistency is smooth and blended to your preference. Divide between glasses and serve.

Calories: 85 Fat: 0g; Chol: 0mg; Sodium: 3mg; Carb: 23g; Fiber: 2g; Protein: 1g

MAKES 1 TO 2 SERVINGS (ABOUT 2 CUPS)

Chocolate Soy Cherry Smoothie

REMINISCENT OF A **CHOCOLATE CHERRY MILKSHAKE**, THIS SMOOTHIE CARRIES ALL THAT AND MORE.

INGREDIENTS

1½ cups chocolate-flavored soy yogurt

1 banana, peeled, cut in half

1 tbsp premium chocolate sauce

1 cup frozen cherries, pitted

DIRECTIONS

Place ingredients into the blender in the order listed. Press Start and increase the power gradually until the ingredients are well-blended. The smoothie is done when the consistency is smooth and blended to your preference. Serve right away.

Calories: 254 Fat: 4g; Chol: 0mg: Sodium: 110mg; Carb: 53g; Fiber: 6g; Protein: 7g

MAKES 2 SERVINGS (ABOUT 2 CUPS)

Cinnamon Pear Smoothie

CINNAMON AND **PEARS**, COMPLEMENTED BY JUST
A HINT OF **VANILLA**, PARTNER IN A RICH SMOOTHIE.

INGREDIENTS

2 ripe pears, peeled and cored

1½ cups nonfat vanilla-flavored yogurt

pinch ground cinnamon

4 ice cubes

DIRECTIONS

Place ingredients into the blender in the order listed. Press Start and increase the power gradually until the ingredients are well-blended. The smoothie is done when the consistency is smooth and blended to your preference. Divide between glasses and serve.

Calories: 223 Fat: 0g; Chol: 4mg; Sodium: 136mg; Carb: 48g; Fiber: 6g; Protein: 9g

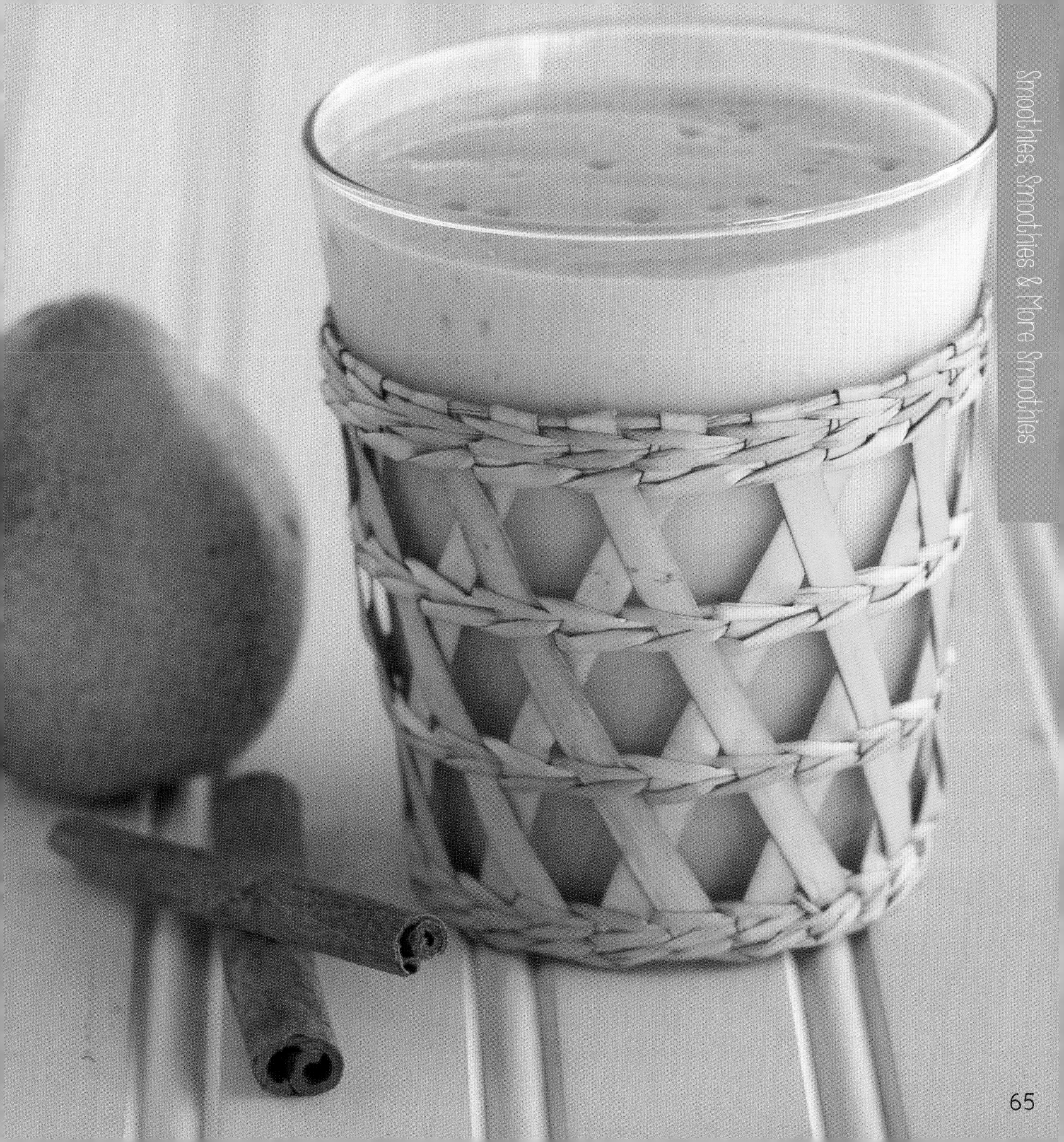

MAKES 2 SERVINGS (ABOUT 2³/4 CUPS)

Caribbean Holiday Smoothie

ADD A LITTLE **FRILLY** UMBRELLA AND YOU'LL **CRUISE** THROUGH THE DAY.

INGREDIENTS

1 cup coconut milk

1 cup frozen pineapple, cut in chunks

1 cup frozen mango, cut in chunks

1 kiwi fruit, peeled

4 ice cubes

DIRECTIONS

Place ingredients into the blender in the order listed. Press Start and increase the power gradually until the ingredients are well-blended. The smoothie is done when the consistency is smooth and blended to your preference. Divide between glasses and serve.

Calories: 349 Fat: 21g; Chol: 0mg; Sodium: 62mg; Carb: 37g; Fiber: 4g; Protein: 3g

MAKES 2 SERVINGS (ABOUT 2½ CUPS)

Honey Dew Cucumber Smoothie

A **SPECIAL BLEND** OF DELICATE FLAVORS
CREATE THIS **REFRESHING** COOLER!

INGREDIENTS

2 tbsp water

1 cucumber, peeled and quartered

½ honeydew melon, peeled, seeded, cut in chunks

6 ice cubes

DIRECTIONS

Place ingredients into the blender in the order listed. Press Start and increase the power gradually until the ingredients are well-blended. The smoothie is done when the consistency is smooth and blended to your preference. Divide between glasses and serve.

Calories: 99 Fat: 1g; Chol: 0mg; Sodium: 47mg; Carb: 25g; Fiber: 3g; Protein: 2g

MAKES 2 TO 3 SERVINGS (ABOUT 2½ CUPS)

Bananas for Blueberries Smoothie

THIS **BALANCED MERGER** CREATES A SIMPLE SMOOTHIE PACKED WITH **WHOLESOME GOODNESS** THAT IS SURE TO BECOME A **FAMILY FAVORITE**.

INGREDIENTS

½ cup unsweetened vanilla almond milk

½ cup blueberry kefir (or use nonfat blueberry yogurt)

1 large banana, peeled, cut in half

1½ cups frozen blueberries

DIRECTIONS

Place ingredients into the blender in the order listed. Press Start and increase the power gradually until the ingredients are well-blended. The smoothie is done when the consistency is smooth and blended to your preference. Serve right away.

Calories: 119 Fat: 1g; Chol: 1mg; Sodium: 47mg; Carb: 27g; Fiber: 4g; Protein: 4g

Chapter 4

Fresh Juices, Cocktails & Purées

**Four Berry Nectar
page 85**

MAKES 1 TO 2 SERVINGS (ABOUT 1³/₄ CUPS)

Tomato Salsa Spinach Juice

RIPE TOMATOES REALLY **POWER UP** AND SHINE IN THIS **MILDLY SPICY** JUICE.

INGREDIENTS

¼ cup water

½ cucumber, peeled and quartered

1½ cups sweet pear tomatoes

1 cup baby spinach, loosely packed

½ lime, juiced

2 tbsp prepared salsa

pinch salt

4 ice cubes

DIRECTIONS

Place ingredients into the blender in the order listed. Press Start and increase the power gradually until the ingredients are well-blended. The juice is done when the consistency is smooth and blended to your preference. Divide between glasses and serve.

Calories: 49 Fat: 1g; Chol: 0mg; Sodium: 165mg; Carb: 7g; Fiber: 7g; Protein: 2g

MAKES 2 SERVINGS (ABOUT 2½ CUPS)

Pineapple, Mango & Fresh Cucumber Juice

MILD CUCUMBER SPARKS THE **TROPICAL FRUIT FLAVORS** IN THIS JUICE.

INGREDIENTS

¼ cup water

1¾ cups pineapple, cut in chunks

1 cucumber, peeled, cut in chunks

1 cup frozen mango, cut in chunks

8 ice cubes

DIRECTIONS

Place ingredients into the blender in the order listed. Press Start and increase the power gradually until the ingredients are well-blended. The juice is done when the consistency is smooth and blended to your preference. Divide between glasses and serve.

Calories: 130 Fat: 1g; Chol: 0mg; Sodium: 4mg; Carb: 34g; Fiber: 4g; Protein: 2g

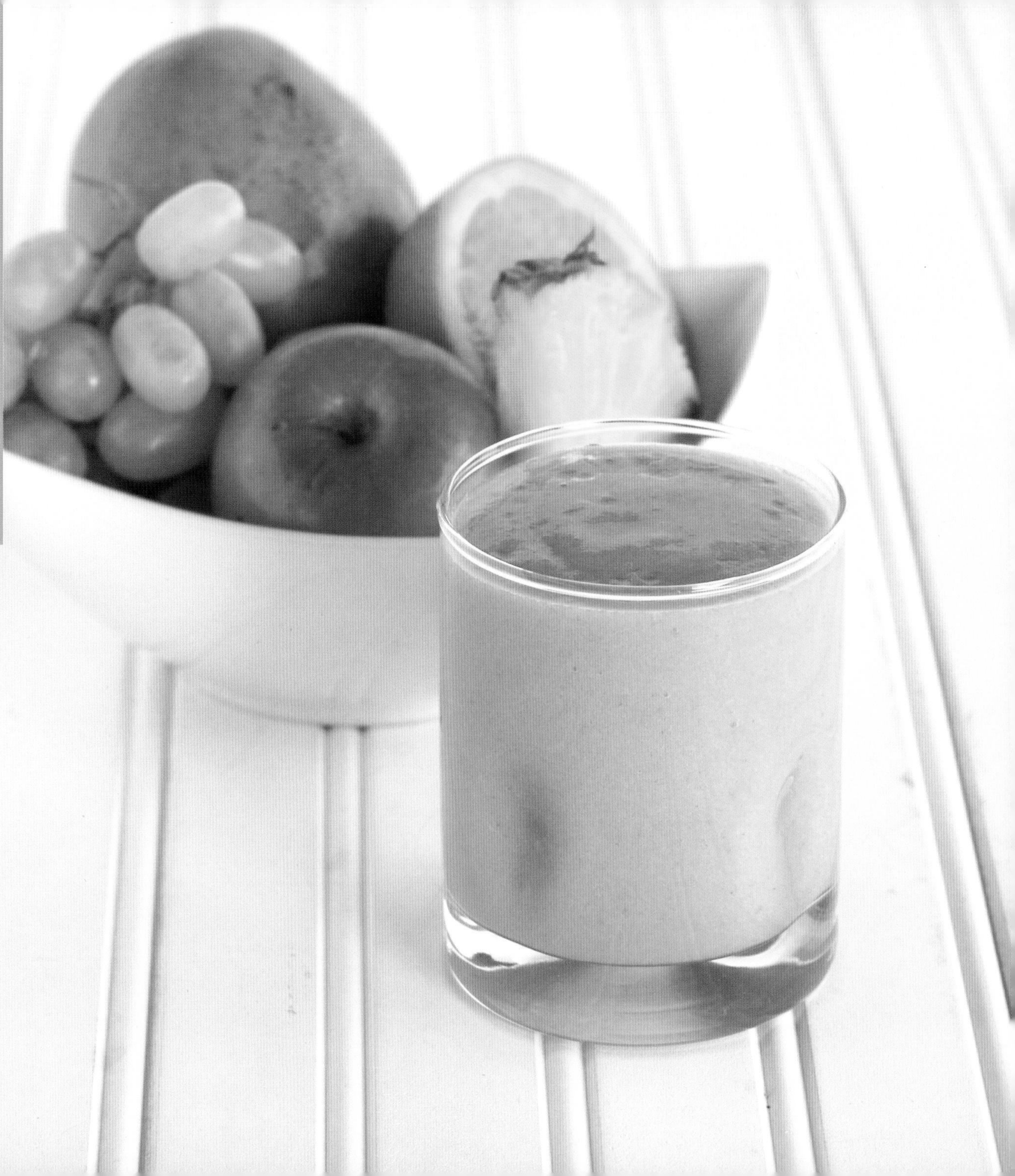

MAKES 6–8 SERVINGS (ABOUT 7 CUPS)

2-Pound Green Whole Juice

ENOUGH **FRESH JUICE** FOR EVERYONE IN YOUR NEIGHBORHOOD!

INGREDIENTS

2 cups green grapes

1 cup mango, cut in chunks

1 orange, peeled, cut in half

½ Granny Smith apple, cut in half

1½ cups fresh pineapple, cut in chunks

1 cup baby spinach leaves, loosely packed

2 cups ice cubes

DIRECTIONS

Place ingredients into the blender in the order listed. Press Start and increase the power gradually until the ingredients are well-blended. The juice is done when the consistency is smooth and blended to your preference. Divide between glasses and serve.

Calories: 57 Fat: 0g; Chol: 1mg; Sodium: 4mg; Carb: 18g; Fiber: 2g; Protein: 1g

MAKES 2 SERVINGS (ABOUT 2¹/₂ CUPS)

Strawberry Supercharge

A **REFRESHING**, ICY TROPICAL JUICE.

INGREDIENTS

¹/₂ cup freshly squeezed orange juice

2 mangos, peeled, cut in chunks

1 cup frozen strawberries

8 ice cubes

DIRECTIONS

Place ingredients into the blender in the order listed. Press Start and increase the power gradually until the ingredients are well-blended. The juice is done when the consistency is smooth and blended to your preference. Divide between glasses and serve.

Calories: 177 Fat: 2g; Chol: 0mg; Sodium: 4mg; Carb: 45g; Fiber: 5g; Protein: 3g

MAKES 1 TO 2 SERVINGS (ABOUT 2½ CUPS)

All Green 24/7 Juice

PEAR AND **KIWI** FRUIT ADD THAT BIT OF SWEETNESS NEEDED WITH **GREENS**. TAKE A LOOK IN YOUR REFRIGERATOR TO **CHANGE UP** INGREDIENTS. USE A VARIETY OF LETTUCES AND OTHER **SWEET FRUIT** TO CREATE COMPLEMENTARY FLAVORS.

INGREDIENTS

1¼ cups Peach & Nectarine Nectar (see recipe p. 78)

1 cup baby spinach, loosely packed

4 leaves romaine lettuce

1 pear, cored, cut in half

1 kiwi fruit, peeled

8 ice cubes

DIRECTIONS

Place ingredients into the blender in the order listed. Press Start and increase the power gradually until the ingredients are well-blended. The juice is done when the consistency is smooth and blended to your preference. Serve at once.

Calories: 177 Fat: 0g; Chol: 0mg; Sodium: 27mg; Carb: 45g; Fiber: 6g; Protein: 2g

MAKES 2 SERVINGS (3 CUPS)

Green Zest Juice

READILY AVAILABLE INGREDIENTS **EASILY CREATE**
THIS INCREDIBLY **TASTY** EVERY-DAY JUICE.

INGREDIENTS

1 cup unfiltered apple juice

1 large cucumber, peeled, cut in half

2 cups baby spinach, loosely packed

2 ribs celery, quartered

½ lemon, peeled

½-inch fresh ginger root, peeled

5 ice cubes

DIRECTIONS

Place ingredients into the blender in the order listed. Press Start and increase the power gradually until the ingredients are well-blended. The juice is done when the consistency is smooth and blended to your preference. Divide between glasses and serve.

Calories: 80 Fat: 0g; Chol: 0mg; Sodium: 45mg; Carb: 19g; Fiber: 2g; Protein: 2g

MAKES 2 SERVINGS (ABOUT 2 3/4 CUPS)

Peach & Nectarine Nectar

USE **VERY RIPE** FRUIT FOR THE MOST SWEETLY
FLAVORED **NECTAR**.

INGREDIENTS

1 cup peach nectar

1 white peach, peeled and pitted

1 nectarine, peeled and pitted

2 ice cubes

DIRECTIONS

Place ingredients into the blender in the order listed. Press Start and increase the power gradually until the ingredients are well-blended. The nectar is done when the consistency is smooth and blended to your preference. Divide between glasses and serve.

Calories: 128 Fat: 1g; Chol: 0mg; Sodium: 9mg; Carb: 33g; Fiber: 3g; Protein: 2g

MAKES 2 TO 4 SERVINGS (ABOUT 3 CUPS)

Fresh Pineapple Field Juice

BLENDED WITH **SELTZER** OR ON ITS OWN, THIS DELIGHTFUL **REFRESHER** IS SURE TO PLEASE.

INGREDIENTS

2 cups fresh pineapple, cut in chunks

2 cups seedless watermelon, cut in chunks

1 lime, peeled

10 ice cubes

DIRECTIONS

Place ingredients into the blender in the order listed. Press Start and increase the power gradually until the ingredients are well-blended. The juice is done when the consistency is smooth and blended to your preference. Divide between glasses and serve.

Calories: 65 Fat: 0g; Chol: 0mg; Sodium: 2mg; Carb: 17g; Fiber: 2g; Protein: 1g

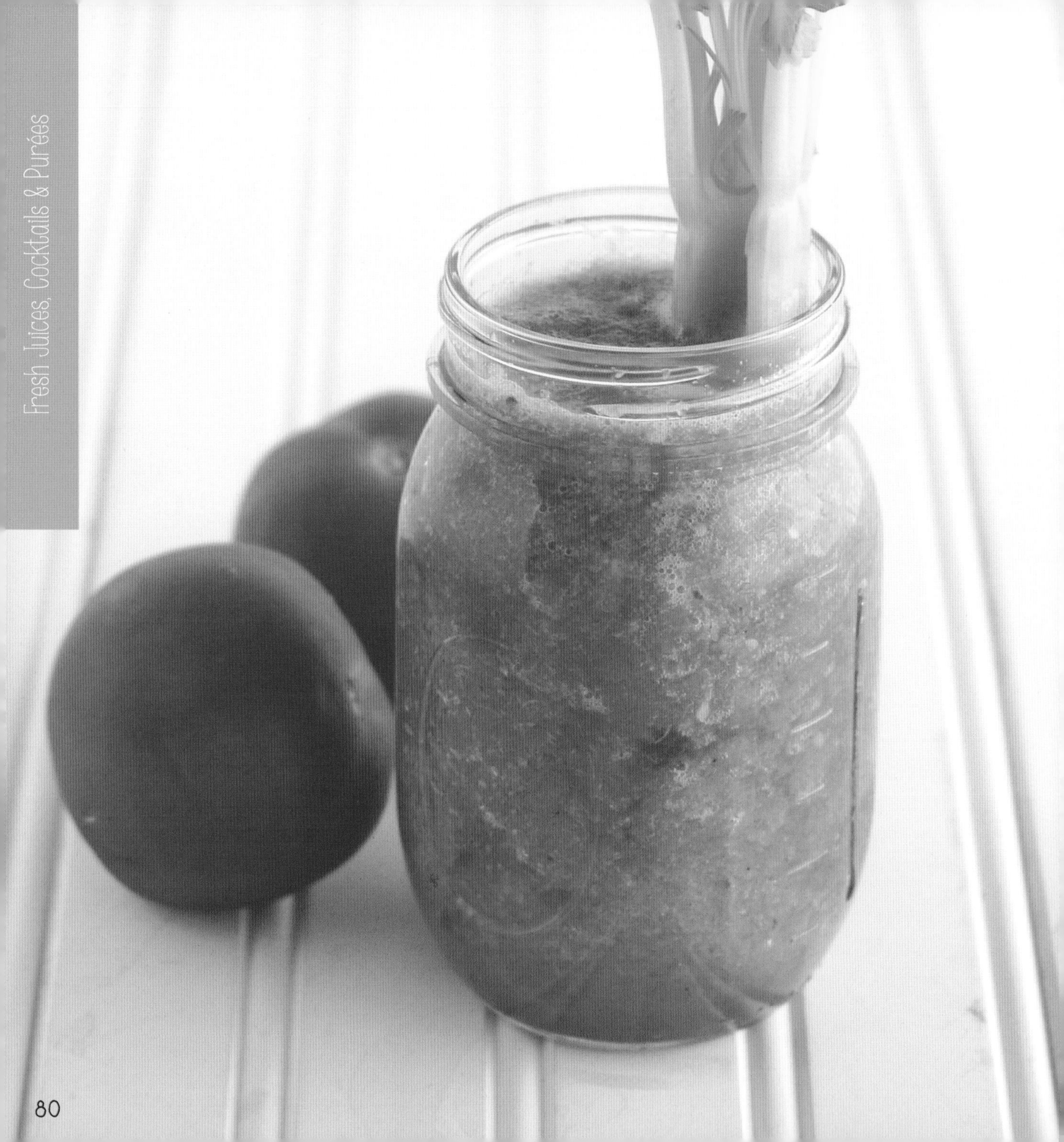

MAKES 1 TO 2 SERVINGS (ABOUT 2 CUPS)

Tomato & Horseradish Juice

THIS VIBRANT JUICE EASILY MORPHS INTO A **BLOODY MARY** WITH THE ADDITION OF A SPLASH OF **VODKA**, DASH OF **CELERY SEED** AND PINCH OF SALT.

INGREDIENTS

½ cup water

2 ripe tomatoes, cored

2 ribs celery, with leaves

1 tsp creamy horseradish

½ lemon, peeled and pith removed

½ jalepeño pepper, with seeds

pinch salt

dash ground black pepper

10 ice cubes

DIRECTIONS

Place ingredients into the blender in the order listed. Press Start and increase the power gradually until the ingredients are well-blended. The juice is done when the consistency is smooth and blended to your preference. Serve right away.

Calories: 29 Fat: 1g; Chol: 0mg; Sodium: 40mg; Carb: 8g; Fiber: 2g; Protein: 1g

MAKES 2 SERVINGS (ABOUT 2½ CUPS)

Fuji Apple & Blueberry Nectar

THE ADDITION OF **FRESH GINGER** GIVES THIS NECTAR A LITTLE SURPRISE **POP**. USE LESS GINGER OR MORE, DEPENDING ON YOUR PREFERENCE.

INGREDIENTS

½ cup apple juice

2 Fuji apples, cored, cut in half

1 cup blueberries

¼-inch fresh ginger root, peeled

DIRECTIONS

Place ingredients into the blender in the order listed. Press Start and increase the power gradually until the ingredients are well-blended. The nectar is done when the consistency is smooth and blended to your preference. Strain, if desired. Divide between glasses and serve.

Calories: 165 Fat: 1g; Chol: 0mg; Sodium: 5mg; Carb: 43g; Fiber: 7g; Protein: 1g

MAKES ABOUT 1¼ CUPS

Papaya Pineapple Purée

THIS LUSCIOUS **TROPICAL BLEND** IS THE PERFECT START TO COCKTAILS, **SAUCES** OR MARINADES.

INGREDIENTS

¾ cup fresh mango, cut in chunks

1 cup fresh papaya, cut in chunks

1 cup fresh pineapple, cut in chunks

½ lime, juiced

DIRECTIONS

Place ingredients into the blender. Press Start and increase power gradually until reaching the highest setting. Blend for 15 seconds. Use as a sauce, marinade or pour into an ice cube tray and freeze until solid. Transfer ice cubes to a self-sealing plastic bag until needed. Freeze for up to 1 month.

Calories: 36 Fat: 0g; Chol: 0mg; Sodium: 2mg; Carb: 10g; Fiber: 1g; Protein: 1g

MAKES 2 SERVINGS (ABOUT 2 CUPS)

Four Berry Nectar

ADD THIS NECTAR TO SMOOTHIES OR BLEND WITH **PLAIN SELTZER** WATER OVER ICE FOR A **THIRST—QUENCHING** DRINK.

INGREDIENTS

½ cup fresh strawberries, hulled

½ cup fresh raspberries

½ cup fresh blackberries

½ cup fresh blueberries

2 tbsp honey (optional)

DIRECTIONS

Place ingredients into the blender in the order listed. Press Start and increase the power gradually until the ingredients are well-blended. The nectar is done when the consistency is smooth and blended to your preference. Strain, if desired. Divide between glasses and serve.

Calories: 129 Fat: 0g; Chol: 0mg; Sodium: 3mg; Carb: 35g; Fiber: 4g; Protein: 2g

MAKES 4 COCKTAILS

Coconut Rum & Pineapple Blast

THIS TROPICAL COCKTAIL SMOOTHIE RESEMBLES A BLENDED **MAI TAI**, WITH THE SAME **DELIGHTFUL** RESULTS.

INGREDIENTS

2½ cups fresh pineapple, cut in chunks

½ cup unsweetened coconut, shredded

1 cup cream of coconut

8 oz coconut-flavored rum

12 ice cubes

4 pineapple wedges for garnish

4 maraschino cherries for garnish

DIRECTIONS

Place ingredients into the blender in the order listed. Press Start and increase the power gradually until the ingredients are well-blended. When ready, the consistency will be smooth and blended to your preference. Divide between ice-filled glasses, garnish each with a pineapple wedge and a cherry and serve immediately.

Calories: 411 Fat: 22g; Chol: 0mg; Sodium: 43mg; Carb: 23g; Fiber: 6g; Protein: 4g

Frozen Strawberry Mint Margaritas

WHEN **SUMMER** STRAWBERRIES ARE IN SEASON, FREEZE ANY **EXTRAS** FOR THESE **SPECTACULAR** MARGARITAS!

INGREDIENTS

½ cup water

½ cup sugar

8 leaves mint

2 cups frozen strawberries

1 cup premium tequila

½ cup lime juice

½ cup triple sec liqueur

8 ice cubes

mint sprigs for garnish

DIRECTIONS

In a small saucepan over medium heat, combine sugar, water and 8 sprigs mint, stirring frequently until sugar is dissolved. Cook for 1 minute and set aside to cool.

When mixture is cooled, remove mint and add the sugar water to the blender. Place remaining ingredients into the blender in the order listed. Press Start and gradually increase power to the highest setting. When smooth, divide between glasses, garnish with mint and serve immediately.

Calories: 202 Fat: 0g; Chol: 0mg; Sodium: 4mg; Carb: 26g; Fiber: 1; Protein:

cook's note:

TO MAKE *top shelf* MARGARITAS, FLOAT TRIPLE SEC *liqueur* ON TOP OF EACH DRINK JUST BEFORE SERVING.

MAKES 1 SERVING (ABOUT 1½ CUPS)

Carrot, Ginger & Orange Juice

FRESH CARROTS ARE **PLEASANTLY SWEET** AND HAVE MANY NUTRITIOUS PROPERTIES. LOOK FOR FIRM, **BRIGHT ORANGE** CARROTS FOR THE BEST JUICE.

INGREDIENTS

¾ cup apple juice

1 orange, peeled, cut in half

1 large carrot, peeled, roughly cut

½-inch fresh ginger root, peeled

10 ice cubes

DIRECTIONS

Place ingredients into the blender in the order listed. Press Start and increase the power gradually until the ingredients are well-blended. The juice is done when the consistency is smooth and blended to your preference. Serve right away.

Calories: 179 Fat: 0g; Chol: 0mg; Sodium: 53mg; Carb: 43g; Fiber: 5g; Protein: 2g

MAKES 8 COCKTAILS

Blackberry Bellinis

A BEAUTIFULLY BRIGHT PLAY ON THE **CLASSIC COCKTAIL** INVENTED AT **HARRY'S BAR** IN VENICE,

INGREDIENTS

1 cup fresh blackberries

2 tbsp granulated sugar

¼ tsp pure vanilla extract

750 ml bottle champagne, preferably prosecco

fresh blackberries for garnish

DIRECTIONS

Place 1 cup blackberries, sugar and vanilla into the blender. Press Start and gradually increase power until blended and smooth. Strain purée through a fine mesh sieve. Place 2 tablespoons of blackberry purée into each champagne flute and carefully add champagne. Garnish each with a blackberry and serve.

Calories: 81 Fat: 0g; Chol: 0mg; Sodium: 0mg; Carb: 6g; Fiber: 1g; Protein: 1g

 **MAKES 4 COCKTAILS**

Cucumber & Orange Gin Ricky

THIS SEDUCTIVE **HIGHBALL** OFFERS A
SECRET **WHOLESOME KICK** WITH THE ADDITION
OF CUCUMBER AND ORANGE JUICE.

INGREDIENTS

½ cucumber, peeled and seeded

½ cup fresh orange juice

¼ cup fresh squeezed lime juice

8 oz gin

8 oz club soda

ice cubes

lime wedges for garnish

DIRECTIONS

Place cucumber, orange juice and lime juice into the blender. Press Start and blend until smooth. Add gin and pulse 4 to 8 times to blend. Divide between 4 ice-filled glasses and top each with a splash of soda. Garnish with lime and serve immediately.

Calories: 171 Fat: 0g; Chol: 0mg; Sodium: 16mg; Carb: 5g; Fiber: 0g; Protein: 0g

MAKES ABOUT 1¼ CUPS

Spinach & Basil Purée

BUSY DAY? **POP A CUBE** OF THIS FROZEN **ALMOST-PESTO** PURÉE INTO SOUPS OR SAUCES AND YOU'RE ON THE WAY TO A DELICIOUSLY **RICH** ENTRÉE.

INGREDIENTS

⅔ cup vegetable broth or water

1 cup baby spinach, loosely packed

1 cup fresh basil, loosely packed

½ cup pine nuts

pinch salt

dash ground black pepper

DIRECTIONS

Place ingredients into the blender in the order listed. Press Start and gradually increase power until purée is smooth. Carefully pour into ice cube tray and freeze until solid. Transfer ice cubes to a self-sealing plastic bag until needed. Freeze for up to 1 month.

Calories: 37 Fat: 3g; Chol: 0mg; Sodium: 45mg; Carb: 1g; Fiber: 0g; Protein: 1g

MAKES ABOUT 1¹/₄ CUPS

Cucumber, Lemon & Ginger Purée

AN **EXOTIC** FUSION, THESE CUBES ARE **MINI BOOSTS** FOR COCKTAILS, SMOOTHIES, JUICES, **COLD SOUPS** AND MORE.

INGREDIENTS

¹/₄ cup water

1 cucumber, peeled and quartered

¹/₂ inch fresh ginger root, peeled

1 lemon, juiced

DIRECTIONS

Place ingredients into the blender in the order listed. Press Start and gradually increase power until smooth. Carefully pour into ice cube tray and freeze until solid. Transfer ice cubes to a self-sealing plastic bag until needed. Freeze for up to 1 month.

Calories: 2 Fat: 0g; Chol: 0mg; Sodium: 0mg; Carb: 1g; Fiber: 0g; Protein: 0g

MAKES 1¹/₄ CUPS

Kona Coffee Purée

A PERFECT ADDITION TO YOUR **MORNING SMOOTHIE**, A CREAMY COCKTAIL OR A FAVORITE **GOURMET** COFFEE.

INGREDIENTS

1 cup brewed Kona coffee, chilled

½ cup cream of coconut

½ cup fresh coconut, shredded (not dehydrated)

DIRECTIONS

Place ingredients into the blender in the order listed. Press Start and increase power to medium speed. Blend for 30 seconds. Carefully pour into ice cube tray and freeze until solid. Transfer ice cubes to a self-sealing plastic bag until needed. Freeze for up to 1 month.

Calories: 36 Fat: 3g; Chol: 0mg; Sodium: 7mg; Carb: 2g; Fiber: 1g; Protein: 0g

**Buffalo Chicken Wings
with Roquefort Dip
page 106**

MAKES 9 TO 16 BARS

Three Seed Fruit Bars

A GREAT LITTLE ENERGY PICK-ME-UP OR BREAKFAST ON THE GO.

INGREDIENTS

½ cup dried apricots

½ cup dried dates, pitted

½ cup dried apple

¼ cup flax seeds

½ cup sunflower seeds

½ cup pumpkin seeds

½ tsp ground cinnamon

1 cup granola

DIRECTIONS

Place all ingredients, except granola, into the blender and press Start. Pulse until just combined, scraping down sides as needed to mix. Add granola and pulse 2 times. Press mixture into a parchment-lined 8-inch square baking pan and refrigerate until firm. Cut into bars or bite-sized squares, as desired.

Calories: 108 Fat: 5g; Chol: 0mg; Sodium: 7mg; Carb: 14g; Fiber: 0g; Protein: 5g

MAKES 12 TO 16 BARS

Coconut Island Bars

TROPICAL **FLAVORS** BLEND DELICIOUSLY WITH
PUFFED RICE CEREAL AND CRUNCHY **SEEDS**.

INGREDIENTS

½ cup dried mango

1 cup dried dates, pitted

½ cup dried pineapple

½ cup shredded unsweetened coconut

½ cup macadamia nuts

½ cup sesame seeds

½ cup almond meal

½ tsp ground cardamom

1 cup puffed rice cereal

DIRECTIONS

Place all ingredients, except puffed rice, into the blender and press Start. Pulse until just combined, scraping down sides as needed to mix. Stir the rice cereal into the mixture by hand. Press into a parchment-lined, 8-inch square baking pan and refrigerate until firm. Cut into bars or bite-sized squares, as desired.

Calories: 167 Fat: 13g; Chol: 0mg; Sodium: 5mg; Carb: 12g; Fiber: 3g; Protein: 3g

MAKES 9 TO 16 BARS

Cherry Chocolate Chip Bars

DESSERT BARS OR **ENERGY BARS**? DEPENDS ON
YOUR **MOOD** OF THE **MOMENT**, DOESN'T IT?

INGREDIENTS

½ cup almonds, toasted

1 cup dried cherries

½ cup dried dates, pitted

½ cup almond butter

1 cup granola

1 cup semi-sweet chocolate chips

DIRECTIONS

Place almonds, cherries, dates and almond butter into the blender and press Start. Pulse until just combined, scraping down sides as needed to mix. Add granola and chocolate chips by hand. Press into a parchment-lined, 8-inch square baking pan and refrigerate until firm. Cut into bars or bite-sized squares, as desired.

Calories: 186 Fat: 10g; Chol: 0mg; Sodium: 5mg; Carb: 24g; Fiber: 2g; Protein: 4g

MAKES 12 TO 18 LEATHERS

Apple Strawberry Fruit Leather

EASY **HOMEMADE** FRUIT LEATHERS ARE JUST THE
THING FOR **LUNCH BOXES** OR AFTER-SCHOOL

INGREDIENTS

3 apples, peeled, cored and
roughly chopped

½ cup fresh strawberries, hulled

2 to 4 tbsp water

2 tbsp lemon juice

DIRECTIONS

Line a 12 x 17-inch baking sheet with parchment paper and set aside. Place all ingredients, including 2 tablespoons water, into blender in order listed. Press Start and gradually increase speed to medium-high. Blend until mixture is a smooth purée, adding up to 2 tablespoons water, if needed. Transfer to a medium saucepan and cook on low heat until the mixture simmers. Stir occasionally as the mixture reduces and is thickened.

Preheat the oven to 200 F°. Pour the purée onto the prepared baking sheet. Spread the mixture with a spatula to one-eighth inch thickness. Place in the oven and bake for 3 to 4 hours, until leather is tacky, but does not stick to your finger. When done, the leather will be pliable and slightly hardened throughout. If needed, continue baking for up to an additional 30 minutes. Remove and cool. When completely cooled, cut the fruit into strips or squares and roll individually. Store in the refrigerator in a self-sealing plastic bag.

Calories: 17 Fat: 0g; Chol: 0mg; Sodium: 0mg; Carb: 5g; Fiber: 1g; Protein: 0g

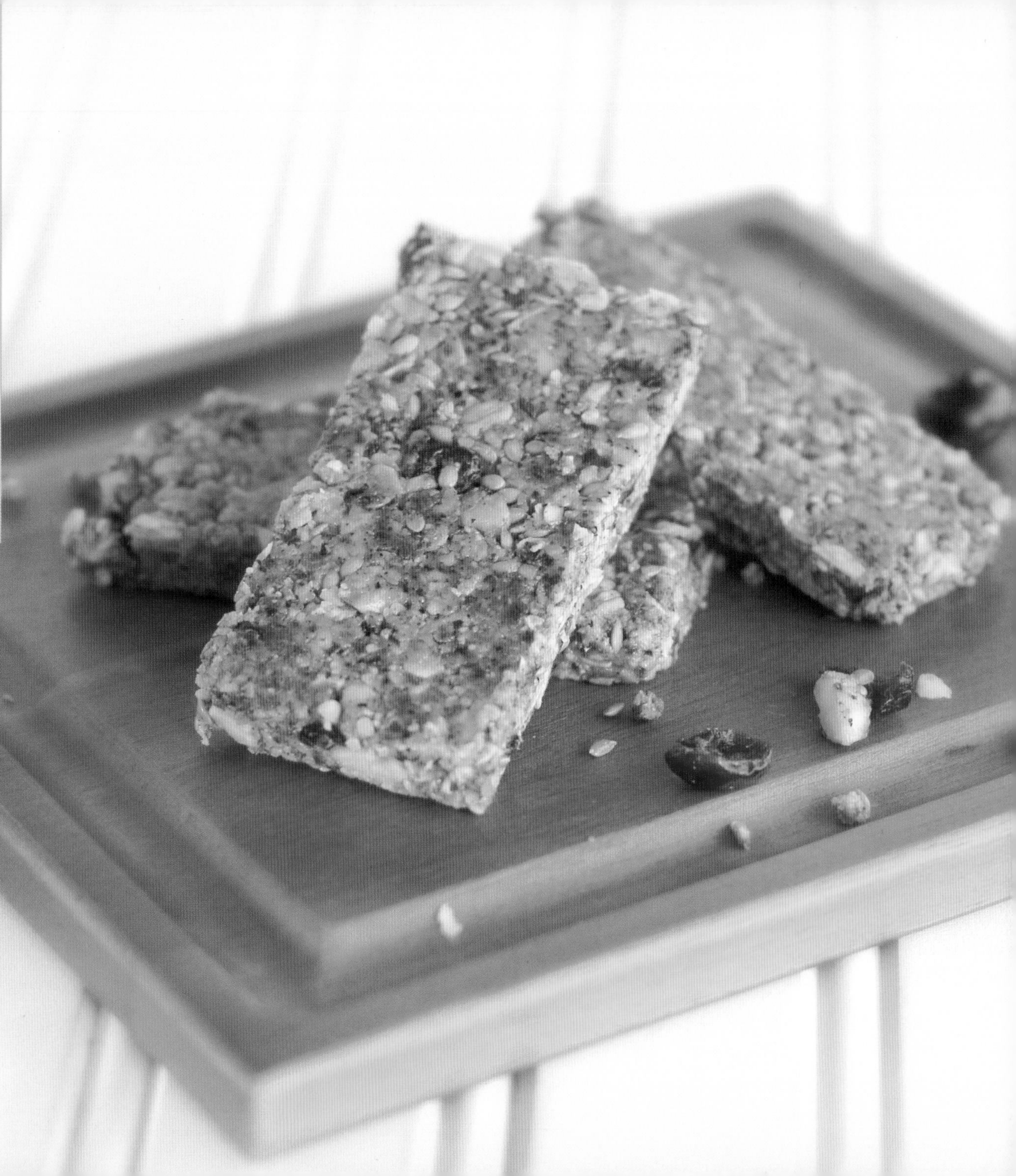

 **MAKES 12 TO 16 BARS**

Nuts for Berry Bars

SUBSTITUTE YOUR **FAVORITE BERRIES** OR NUTS TO MAKE THIS YOUR OWN UNIQUE BLEND. **CHIA SEEDS** ARE A NICE ADDITION.

INGREDIENTS

½ cup hazelnuts

½ cup walnuts

½ cup dried cranberries

½ cup freeze-dried blueberries

½ cup freeze-dried strawberries

¼ cup ground flax seeds

½ cup almond butter, warmed

¼ cup honey

¾ cup regular or quick-cooking oats, uncooked (do not use instant oatmeal)

DIRECTIONS

Place all ingredients into the blender and press Start. Pulse until just combined, scraping down sides as needed to mix. Line an 8 x 8-inch baking pan with parchment paper. Press mixture into pan and refrigerate until firm. Cut into bars or bite-sized squares.

Calories: 197 Fat: 11g; Chol: 0mg; Sodium: 3mg; Carb: 24g; Fiber: 4g; Protein: 4g

MAKES 12 TO 18 LEATHERS

Mango Pineapple Fruit Leather

EVEN YOUR **MOST DEMANDING CRITIC** WILL ENJOY

THESE DELIGHTFULLY FLAVORED FRUIT LEATHERS.

INGREDIENTS

2 fresh mangos, pitted, peeled and roughly cut

½ cup fresh pineapple, cut in chunks

2 to 4 tbsp water

DIRECTIONS

Line a 12 x 17-inch baking pan with parchment paper and set aside. Place the mangoes, pineapple and 2 tablespoons in the blender and press Start. Gradually increase speed to high and blend until the mixture is a smooth purée. If needed, add up to 2 tablespoons water to blend. Transfer the mixture to a medium saucepan and cook over low heat, stirring occasionally, until the mixture is reduced and thickened.

Preheat the oven to 200 F. Pour the purée onto the prepared baking sheet and spread with a spatula to one-eighth inch thickness. Place in the oven and bake for 3 to 4 hours, until leather is tacky, but does not stick to your finger. When done, the leather will be pliable on the edges and slightly hardened throughout. Bake up to an additional 30 minutes, if needed. Remove and cool. When completely cooled, cut the fruit into strips or squares and roll individually. Store in the refrigerator in a self-sealing plastic bag.

Calories: 16 Fat: 0g; Chol: 0mg; Sodium: 0mg; Carb: 4g; Fiber: 0g; Protein: 0g

MAKES ABOUT 2³/₄ CUPS

Paleo Seed & Nut Granola

TOASTED WITH A **HINT OF MAPLE**, THIS GRANOLA CAN BE TOSSED OVER **YOGURT** AND FRUIT, ADDED TO A PARFAIT, OR ENJOYED WITH **ALMOND MILK** IN THE MORNING. A **NATURALLY SWEET** INDULGENCE!

INGREDIENTS

1 cup walnuts

1 cup sunflower seeds

½ cup pumpkin seeds

¼ cup chia seeds

½ cup flax seeds

3 tbsp coconut oil

3 tbsp pure maple syrup

pinch salt

DIRECTIONS

Line a 12 x 17-inch baking pan with parchment paper and set aside. Place all ingredients into blender and press Start. Pulse briefly until the mixture is chunky-smooth, scraping down the sides as needed.

Preheat oven to 300°F. Spread mixture evenly on the prepared baking pan and bake for 10 minutes. Remove granola from oven and stir with a fork, breaking up any large pieces. Return to oven and continue baking for an additional 10 minutes, stirring mixture occasionally. (If you prefer a more pronounced baked flavor, continue baking for 10 minutes.) Cool completely and store in an airtight container for up to 2 weeks.

Calories: 478 Fat: 40g; Chol: 0mg; Sodium: 31; Carb: 23g; Fiber: 10g; Protein: 14g

103

MAKES ABOUT 5¹/₂ CUPS

Moroccan Baked Muesli

START YOUR DAY WITH THE **FLAVORS** OF THE **OASIS**.

INGREDIENTS

1 cup almonds, shelled

1 cup hazelnuts, shelled

2 cups regular or quick-cooking oats, uncooked (do not use instant oatmeal)

¹/₂ cup orange juice

¹/₄ cup agave nectar

3 tbsp canola oil

1 tsp pure vanilla extract

1 tsp ground cardamom

¹/₂ cup goji berries

¹/₂ cup dates, pitted, finely chopped

¹/₂ cup dried apple, finely chopped

DIRECTIONS

Preheat oven to 300°F. Place almonds and hazelnuts into blender and press Start. Pulse to chop evenly. Transfer nuts to a large mixing bowl and add oats. Set aside.

Line a 9 x 13-inch baking sheet with parchment paper and set aside. Place orange juice, agave, canola oil, vanilla and cardamom into blender and press Start. Gradually increase speed to medium until mixture is well-combined. Pour mixture over nuts and oats, tossing well to coat. Spread muesli evenly on the prepared baking sheet and bake for 10 minutes. Remove mixture from oven and stir with a fork, breaking up any large pieces. Return to oven and continue baking for an additional 10 minutes, stirring mixture occasionally. Cool completely and mix with remaining ingredients. Store in an airtight container for up to two weeks.

Calories: 378 Fat: 19g; Chol: 0mg; Sodium: 23mg; Carb: 46g; Fiber: 8g; Protein: 10g

MAKES 24 POTSTICKERS

Chicken & Chinese Vegetable Potstickers

FRESH, HOMEMADE **POTSTICKERS** ARE A **WORLD AWAY** FROM THE FROZEN VARIETY. PREP EVERYTHING AHEAD OF TIME AND **SAUTÉ** WHILE GUESTS ARE WAITING, **FORKS IN HAND**.

INGREDIENTS

4 green onions, trimmed, roughly cut

½ cup Napa cabbage, roughly chopped

6 oz ground chicken

⅓ cup water chestnuts, roughly chopped

1 tbsp fresh ginger, grated

1 tbsp soy sauce

1 tbsp mirin

1 tsp toasted sesame oil

¼ tsp garlic chili sauce

24 square wonton wrappers

¼ cup canola oil, plus more if needed

1 cup chicken broth, divided

soy sauce for table

DIRECTIONS

Place green onions and cabbage into blender. Add water to cover vegetables and press Start. Pulse a few times to chop. Drain water and add chicken, water chestnuts, ginger, soy sauce, mirin, sesame oil and garlic sauce. Press Start and Pulse a few times to combine, scraping down sides as needed.

Spoon mixture by teaspoons into center of each wonton wrapper. Moisten edges with water, fold one corner of wonton over onto opposite corner and gently press edges to seal. Heat 2 tablespoons oil in a large skillet over medium-high heat. When oil is hot, add enough potstickers to fill the pan without over-crowding, and sauté until bottoms are golden brown. Add one-half cup broth, cover pan, reduce heat to medium and simmer for 5 minutes. Uncover pan and continue cooking until liquid has evaporated. Transfer potstickers to serving platter and keep warm. Repeat with remaining potstickers and filling. Serve hot with soy sauce, if desired.

Calories: 123 Fat: 7g; Chol: 23mg; Sodium: 26mg; Carb: 10g; Fiber: 1g; Protein: 5

105

MAKES 8 TO 12 SERVINGS

Buffalo Chicken Wings with Roquefort Dip

A **CLASSIC PUB**-FOOD PLEASER WITH A LUSCIOUS ROQUEFORT **DIPPING** SAUCE.

INGREDIENTS

1 cup lowfat sour cream

½ cup lowfat mayonnaise

2 tbsp lemon juice

½ tsp onion powder

½ tsp garlic powder

½ tsp salt

½ tsp ground black pepper

2 oz Roquefort cheese

½ cup butter

¼ cup bottled hot sauce

¼ cup bottled barbeque sauce

1 cup canola oil

4 lbs chicken wings, patted very dry

8 ribs celery, trimmed and cut into thirds

DIRECTIONS

Place sour cream, mayonnaise, lemon juice, onion powder, garlic powder, salt and pepper into blender in order listed and press Start. Gradually increase speed to medium-high and blend until well-combined. Add Roquefort and gradually increase speed to medium, blending until smooth. Transfer to bowl and cover. Chill for at least 1 hour.

Melt butter in a medium saucepan over medium heat. Whisk in hot sauce and barbeque sauce. Simmer for 1 minute, whisking occasionally, and transfer to a large mixing bowl. Set aside.

Heat oil in a deep, large skillet over medium-high heat. When oil is 375°F, fry chicken in batches until crispy and golden brown, about 6 to 8 minutes. Chicken is done when no pink remains and the internal temperature is 160°F. Remove with slotted spoon and drain on a paper towel-lined plate. Using tongs, place the wings in the butter barbeque sauce and lightly toss to coat. Serve immediately with Roquefort cheese dip and celery sticks.

Calories: 475 Fat: 23g; Chol: 127mg; Sodium: 509mg; Carb: 7g; Fiber: 0g; Protein: 30g

MAKES 8 TO 10 SERVINGS

Swiss Cheese Spread with French Bread Bites

THIS LUSCIOUS, RICH SPREAD IS PACKED WITH CLASSIC BACON AND CHEESE FLAVORS. SERVE WITH BAGUETTE SLICES, BUTTERY CRACKERS OR STEAMED ARTICHOKES.

INGREDIENTS

8 oz whipped cream cheese, at room temperature

½ cup Swiss cheese, shredded

¼ cup mayonnaise

2 tbsp white wine

3 slices bacon, cooked crisp, crumbled

2 green onions, minced

1 French bread baguette, cut into 1-inch cubes

DIRECTIONS

Place cream cheese, Swiss cheese, mayonnaise and wine into blender and press Start. Gradually increase speed to high and blend until very smooth, about 1 minute. Transfer to a serving bowl and add the bacon and green onions, stirring a few times to mix well. Cover tightly and chill for 1 hour before serving. Serve with French bread cubes.

Calories: 158 Fat: 14g; Chol: 33mg; Sodium: 213mg; Carb: 5g; Fiber: 0g; Protein: 4g

MAKES 4 TO 6 SERVINGS

Baba Ganoush

THIS SMOKY, GARLICKY SPREAD CALLS OUT FOR TOASTED PITA BREAD OR SLICED FRESH VEGETABLES. TRY USING IT AS A SPREAD IN HEARTY SANDWICHES IN PLACE OF MAYONNAISE.

INGREDIENTS

1 large eggplant, baked until softened

2 cloves garlic, roasted and peeled

2 tbsp tahini (sesame seed paste)

2 tbsp olive oil, divided

2 tbsp lemon juice

½ tsp ground cumin

½ tsp salt

2 tbsp flat leaf parsley, minced

DIRECTIONS

Cut eggplant in half and scoop pulp into blender. Add garlic, tahini, 1 tablespoon oil, lemon juice, cumin and salt and process until smooth. Transfer to a serving bowl and drizzle with remaining olive oil. Sprinkle with parsley to garnish.

Calories: 84 Fat: 8g; Chol: 0mg; Sodium: 197mg; Carb: 5g; Fiber: 2g; Protein: 2g

Spicy Tropical Fruit Salsa with Chile Lime Tortilla Triangles

ADD **MARIACHIS** AND DANCE THE NIGHT AWAY!

INGREDIENTS

5 6-inch corn tortillas

2 tbsp coconut oil

4 tbsp lime juice, divided

¼ tsp red chile powder

1 cup fresh pineapple, cut in chunks

1 mango, peeled, cut in chunks

1 papaya, peeled, cut in chunks

¼ red onion, peeled, roughly chopped

1 small jalapeño pepper, seeded and quartered

¼ tsp fine sea salt

2 tbsp fresh cilantro leaves

DIRECTIONS

Preheat oven to 350°F. Use a pastry brush to paint tortillas with oil. Brush tortillas with one-half of the lime juice, then sprinkle with chile powder. Cut each tortilla into 6 wedges. Place on a baking sheet and bake until crispy, about 15 minutes.

Place pineapple, mango, papaya, onion and pepper into blender. Press Start and Pulse until the salsa is combined to desired consistency. Add remaining lime juice and salt and Pulse again. Scoop salsa into a serving bowl and garnish with cilantro. Serve with the tortilla triangles.

Calories: 126 Fat: 5g; Chol: 0mg; Sodium: 103mg; Carb: 19g; Fiber: 2g; Protein: 1g

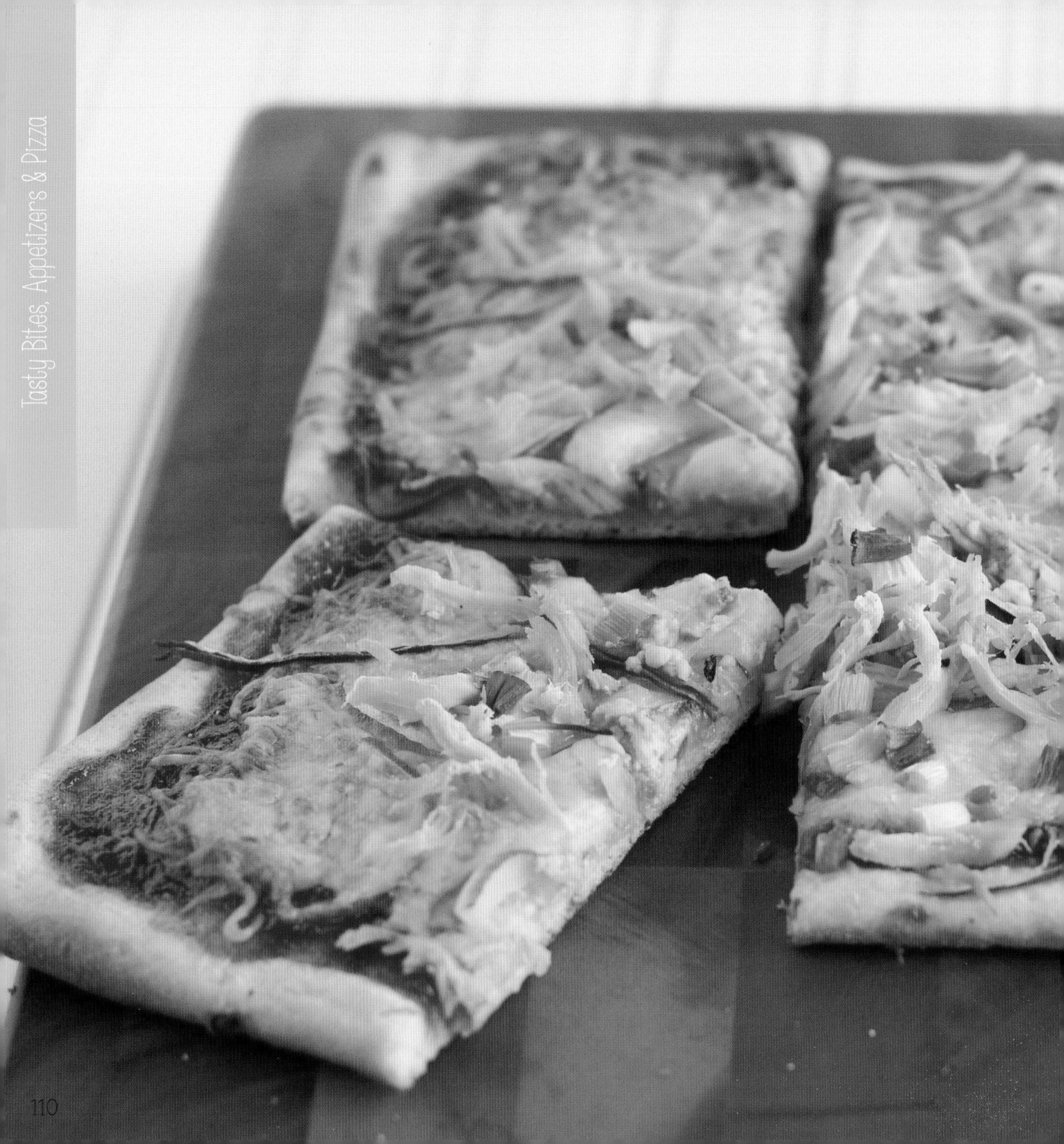

MAKES 1 PIZZA

Barbecue Chicken Pizza

A HANDS-DOWN **FAVORITE** FOR ANY **CASUAL** GATHERING.

INGREDIENTS

¾ cup bottled barbeque sauce

¼ cup tomato paste

3 cloves garlic, peeled

1 tbsp olive oil

½ tsp red pepper flakes

1 recipe Basic Pizza Dough (see recipe p. 112) (or use a purchased dough)

1½ cups mozzarella cheese, shredded

8 oz grilled or roasted chicken, shredded

½ red onion, peeled, thinly sliced

2 green onions, chopped

¼ cup blue cheese, crumbled

DIRECTIONS

Preheat oven to 450°F. Place barbeque sauce, tomato paste, garlic, oil and red pepper into the blender and press Start. Gradually increase the speed to medium high and blend until smooth. Set aside.

On a lightly floured surface, roll out dough to one-half inch thickness and transfer to pizza pan. Spread pizza sauce evenly over dough, leaving a one-fourth inch border around the edge. Scatter mozzarella cheese over sauce and layer with chicken, red and green onions. Sprinkle the blue cheese over all. Bake until cheese is melted and crust is golden brown, about 10 to 12 minutes. Slice and serve.

Calories: 273 Fat: 12g; Chol: 49mg; Sodium: 822mg; Carb: 26g; Fiber: 1g; Protein: 19g

Tasty Bites, Appetizers & Pizza

Basic Pizza Dough

CHEWY, YUMMY, HOMEMADE!

INGREDIENTS

1 cup water, warmed to 110-115°F

¼ oz pkg active dry yeast

1 tsp granulated sugar

2 tbsp olive oil

2¼ cups all-purpose white flour, divided

1 tsp salt

DIRECTIONS

Place water, yeast, sugar and oil into blender and set aside until foamy, about 5 minutes. When foamy, press Start and Pulse briefly to combine. Add 1 cup flour and salt and Pulse again just until combined. Add remaining flour in one-fourth cup increments, Pulsing to form a sticky dough. Transfer to a lightly oiled bowl and turn to coat all sides. Let rise until doubled in size, about 30 to 45 minutes. Roll out dough and bake according to recipe.

Calories: 84 Fat: 1g; Chol: 0mg; Sodium: 147mg; Carb: 17g; Fiber: 1g; Protein: 3g

Roasted Corn & Green Chile Pizza

SLICE INTO **THIN STRIPS** TO CREATE AN APPETIZER PIZZA OR SERVE AS AN **ENTRÉE**. EITHER WAY, **EAST MEETS SOUTHWEST** IN THIS DELIGHTFUL PIZZA.

INGREDIENTS

8 oz ground turkey

1 tsp dried oregano

½ tsp ground cumin

¼ tsp cayenne pepper

½ tsp salt, divided

½ tsp ground black pepper

1 cup Blender White Sauce
(see recipe p. 189)

4 oz can diced green chilies

1 Basic Pizza Dough
(see recipe p. 112)

1 cup Colby Jack cheese, shredded

½ cup cojita cheese, crumbled

½ cup white corn, roasted (or use canned white or yellow corn)

2 tbsp fresh cilantro leaves, chopped

DIRECTIONS

Preheat oven to 450°F. In a sauté pan over medium-high heat, sauté turkey, oregano, cumin, cayenne pepper and one-fourth teaspoon salt until cooked through and crumbly, breaking up large pieces with the back of a wooden spoon. Drain any juices and set aside.

In a small bowl, combine Blender White Sauce with the green chilies and set aside.

On a lightly floured surface, roll out dough to one-half inch thickness and transfer to pizza pan. Spread green chile sauce evenly over dough, leaving a one-fourth inch border around the edge. Scatter cheeses, turkey mixture, corn and cilantro over pizza. Bake pizza until cheese is melted and crust is golden brown, about 10 to 12 minutes. Slice and serve.

Calories: 253 Fat: 13g; Chol: 46mg; Sodium: 651mg; Carb: 23g; Fiber: 1g; Protein: 13g

cook's note:

SUBSTITUTE COOKED, SHREDDED PORK OR *chicken* FOR THE TURKEY, IF DESIRED.

MAKES 10 TO 12 SERVINGS

Greek Skordalia Sauce (Potato Garlic Dip)

A HEARTY ADDITION TO A **WINTERTIME PARTY**. SERVE A SMALL SCOOP WITH **PORK OR BEEF SLIDERS** FOR A UNIQUE TWIST ON THE **TRADITIONAL SIDE DISH** OF FRENCH FRIES.

INGREDIENTS

¾ cup olive oil

¾ cup blanched almonds

8 cloves garlic, peeled

¼ cup lemon juice

1 tbsp white wine vinegar

2 large russet potatoes, peeled, boiled whole

½ tsp salt

DIRECTIONS

Place oil, almonds, garlic, lemon juice and vinegar into blender and press Start. Gradually increase speed to medium and blend until very smooth, about 1 minute. Mash potatoes in a large bowl. Add the almond mixture and salt, stirring until well-mixed. Serve while warm.

Calories: 206 Fat: 17g; Chol: 0mg; Sodium: 101mg; Carb: 13g; Fiber: 2g; Protein: 3g

Maple Carrot Soup,
page 122

MAKES 4 SERVINGS

Garden Gazpacho

GAZPACHO HAS BEEN A **FAVORITE SOUP** FOR THE PAST
FIVE **DECADES**, EVER SINCE SOME ENTERPRISING WOMAN
REALIZED HER **GARDEN BOUNTY** HAD OVERRUN THE ENTIRE YARD.

INGREDIENTS

2 large ripe tomatoes, cored, quartered

1 cucumber, peeled, cut in half

½ green bell pepper, cored, seeded, roughly cut

½ red onion, peeled

2 green onions, cut in half

2 cloves garlic, peeled

¼ bunch flat leaf parsley, stems removed

¼ bunch cilantro, stems removed

½ cup red wine

¼ cup water

1 tbsp red or white wine vinegar

1 tbsp olive oil

1 tsp ground paprika

1 tsp ground black pepper

½ tsp kosher salt

garlic-flavored croutons for garnish

DIRECTIONS

Combine vegetables and herbs in a large bowl. Transfer half of mixture into blender and Pulse until mixture is chunky-smooth. Add red wine, water, vinegar, oil, paprika, pepper and salt and gradually increase speed to medium-low. Blend for 30 seconds and add remaining vegetable mixture. Pulse just until combined. Cover and refrigerate until well-chilled, at least 1 hour. Taste and adjust seasonings. Garnish each serving with garlic croutons.

Calories: 79 Fat: 3g; Chol: 0mg; Sodium: 292mg; Carb: 4g; Fiber: 1g; Protein: 1g

MAKES 4 TO 6 SERVINGS

Spicy & Icy Avocado Salsa Soup

SERVE THIS **ICY** SOUP ALONGSIDE HOT, **CHEESY CHICKEN** ENCHILADAS.

INGREDIENTS

2 ripe avocados, halved, pitted and peeled

4 oz can diced roasted green chilies

½ white onion, peeled

3 cups vegetable broth

½ cup lowfat sour cream

¼ cup fresh lime juice

¾ tsp salt

½ tsp black pepper

½ cup prepared roasted tomato salsa

DIRECTIONS

Place avocados, green chilies, onion and vegetable broth into blender and press Start. Gradually increase speed to medium-low and blend until smooth. Add the sour cream, juice, salt and pepper and Pulse until smooth. Transfer to an airtight container and refrigerate until well-chilled, at least 1 hour. Serve topped with a spoonful of salsa for garnish.

Calories: 163 Fat: 13g; Chol: 7mg; Sodium: 892mg; Carb: 12g; Fiber: 6g; Protein: 3g

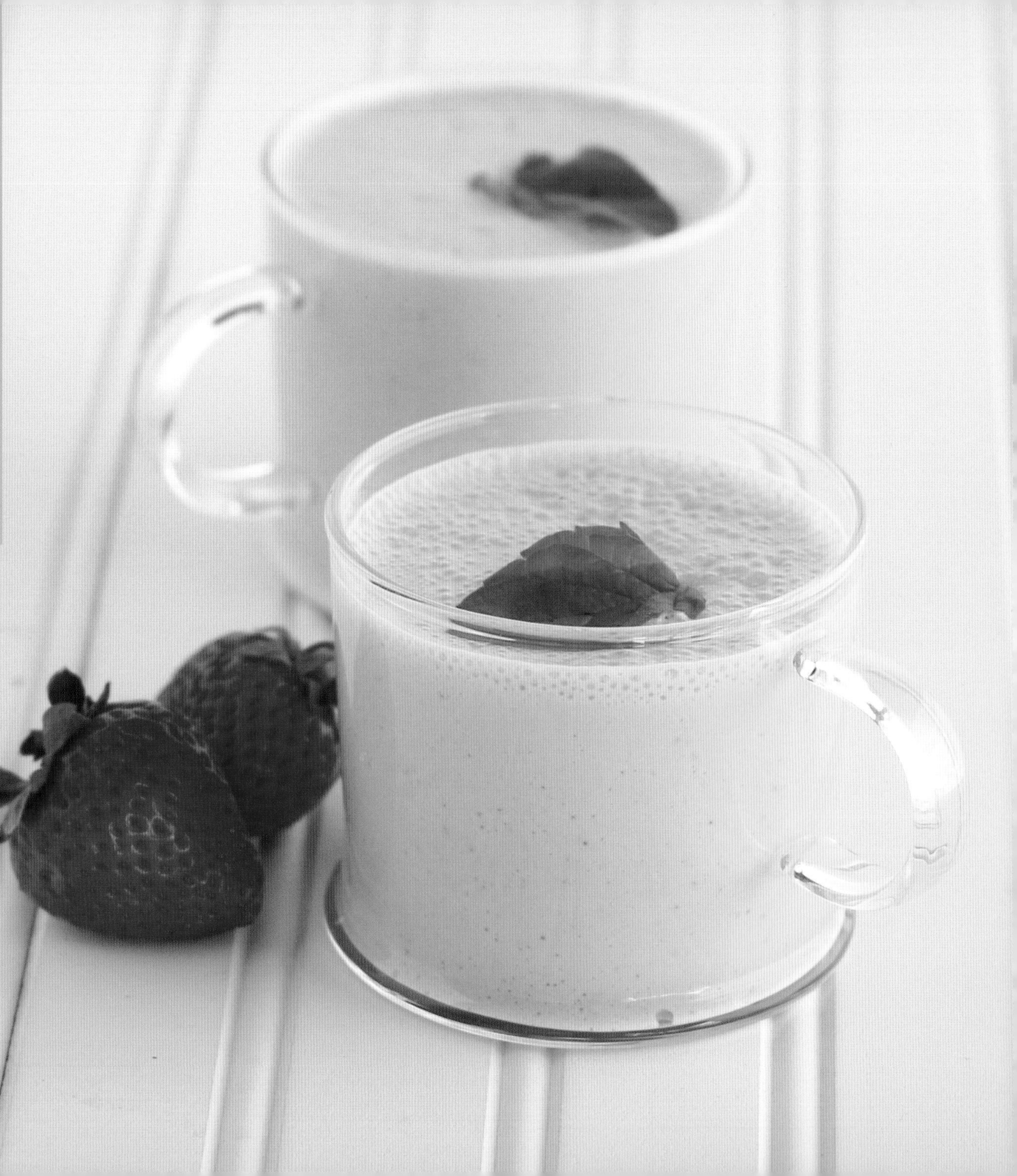

MAKES 4 SERVINGS

Summer Strawberry Soup

FAIRLY **ELEGANT** AND NICE ENOUGH TO SERVE TO **LADIES WHO GATHER** FOR LUNCH.

INGREDIENTS

2 cups frozen strawberries

1 cup lowfat sour cream

1 cup lowfat plain Greek yogurt

1 cup crisp white wine

4 fresh mint sprigs for garnish

DIRECTIONS

Place strawberries, sour cream, yogurt and wine into blender and press Start. Gradually increase speed to medium and blend until smooth, 1 to 2 minutes. Serve immediately, garnished with mint sprigs.

Calories: 182 Fat: 6g; Chol: 26mg; Sodium: 88mg; Carb: 16g; Fiber: 2g; Protein: 10g

MAKES 4 SERVINGS

Non-Dairy Cream of Broccoli Soup

A LUSH **VEGAN** INTERPRETATION OF CREAMY BROCCOLI SOUP.
YOU **WILL NOT MISS** THE CREAM.

INGREDIENTS

1½ **cups raw cashews**

1 **tbsp olive oil**

2 **cups fresh broccoli, cut in florets**

½ **yellow onion, peeled and chopped**

4 **cups vegetable broth**

¾ **tsp salt**

½ **tsp ground black pepper**

DIRECTIONS

Place cashews in a medium bowl and add enough water to cover. Soak cashews in water for at least 2 hours. Drain, discard water and set cashews aside.

Heat oil in a stockpot over medium heat. Add onion and sauté until softened, stirring often. Add one-half cup vegetable broth and broccoli and simmer until broccoli is tender-crisp, about 5 minutes.

Place drained cashews and three-fourths cup vegetable broth into blender and press Start. Gradually increase speed to high and blend until smooth. Add cooked broccoli mixture and remaining broth and continue blending until smooth. Taste and add seasonings to taste. Serve hot, at room temperature, or chilled.

Calories: 330 Fat: 27g; Chol: 0mg; Sodium: 1535mg; Carb: 23g; Fiber: 3g; Protein: 9g

 **MAKES 4 SERVINGS**

Roasted Root Vegetable Soup with Smoky Paprika

SMOKED **HUNGARIAN PAPRIKA** MAKES ALL

THE DIFFERENCE IN THIS FLAVORFUL SOUP.

INGREDIENTS

4 cloves garlic, peeled

2 cups butternut squash, cubed

1 rib celery, cut into thirds

½ yellow onion, peeled

2 tbsp olive oil

2 tsp smoked Hungarian paprika

½ tsp kosher salt

½ tsp ground black pepper

4 cups vegetable broth

sour cream for garnish

DIRECTIONS

Preheat oven to 400°F. Line an oven-proof 9 x 13-inch baking pan with parchment paper and add the garlic, squash, celery and onion. Toss with oil, paprika, salt and pepper to coat. Roast until tender, about 20-30 minutes. Cool vegetables slightly and transfer to blender. Add vegetable broth and press Start. Gradually increase speed to medium-high and blend until smooth. Heat on the stovetop, if desired, or serve at room temperature. Garnish each serving with a small dollop of sour cream before serving.

Calories: 107 Fat: 6g; Chol: 0mg; Sodium: 1341mg; Carb: 11g; Fiber: 2g; Protein: 1g

MAKES 6 SERVINGS

Maple Carrot Soup

SAUTÉING THE CARROTS IN **BUTTER** ADDS A LUSCIOUS RICHNESS, **ELEVATING** THE **FLAVORS** OF THIS DELICIOUS SOUP!

INGREDIENTS

¼ cup butter

4 carrots, peeled and sliced

2 tbsp maple syrup

¼ tsp ground ginger

½ tsp salt

½ tsp white pepper

6 cups chicken or vegetable broth

DIRECTIONS

In a large heavy-bottomed skillet, melt butter over medium-high heat. When sizzling, add carrots, reduce heat to medium and sauté, stirring frequently until softened and golden brown around edges. Stir in maple syrup, ginger, salt and pepper and cook for a minute or two longer to incorporate flavors. Add broth and bring to a simmer. Remove pan from heat and, when cool enough to handle, transfer contents to blender and press Start. Gradually increase speed to high and blend until very smooth. If desired, return soup to stockpot to re-heat for a few minutes or serve as is.

Calories: 128 Fat: 9g; Chol: 25g; Sodium: 1094mg; Carb: 11g; Fiber: 2g; Protein: 2g

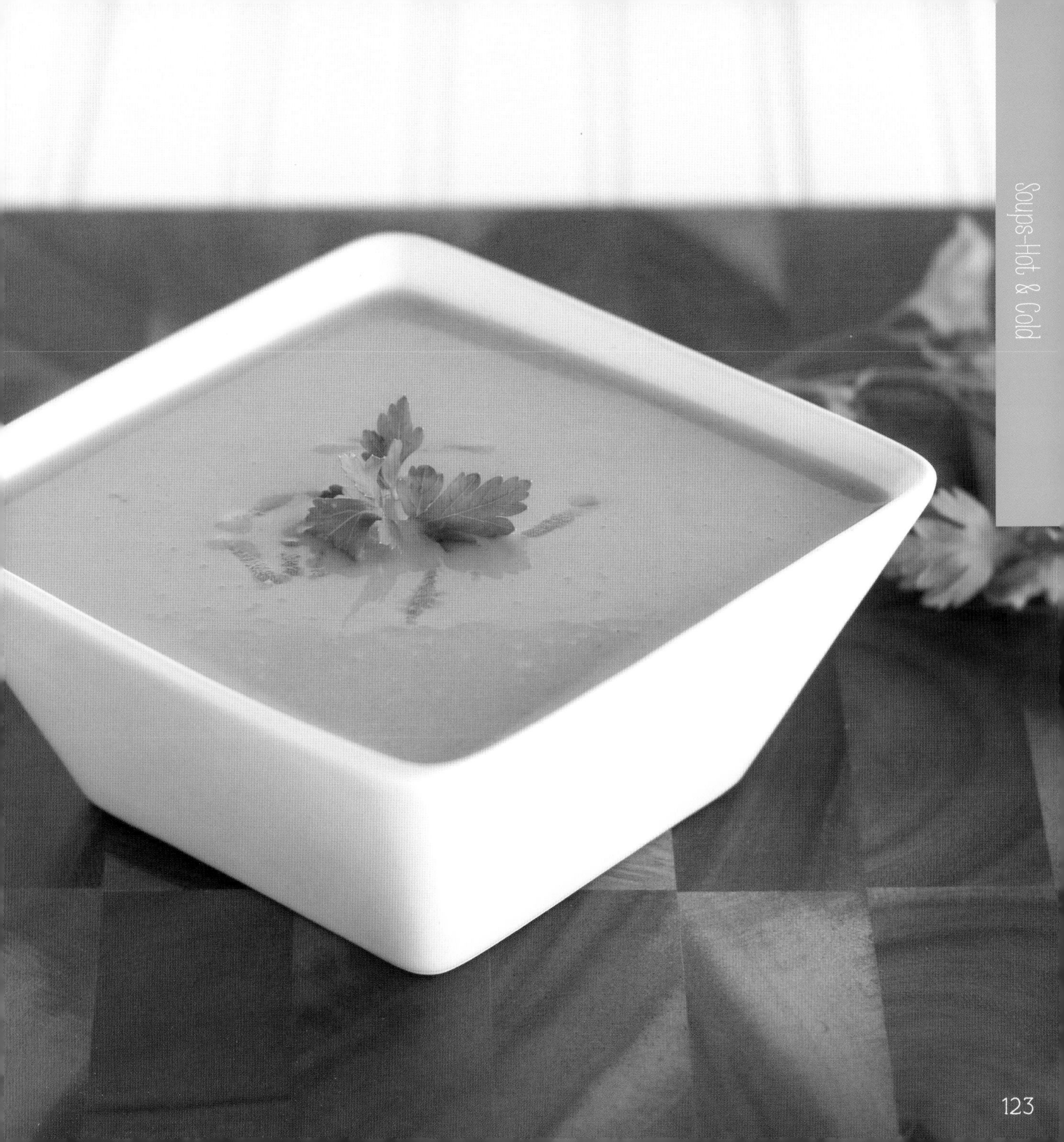

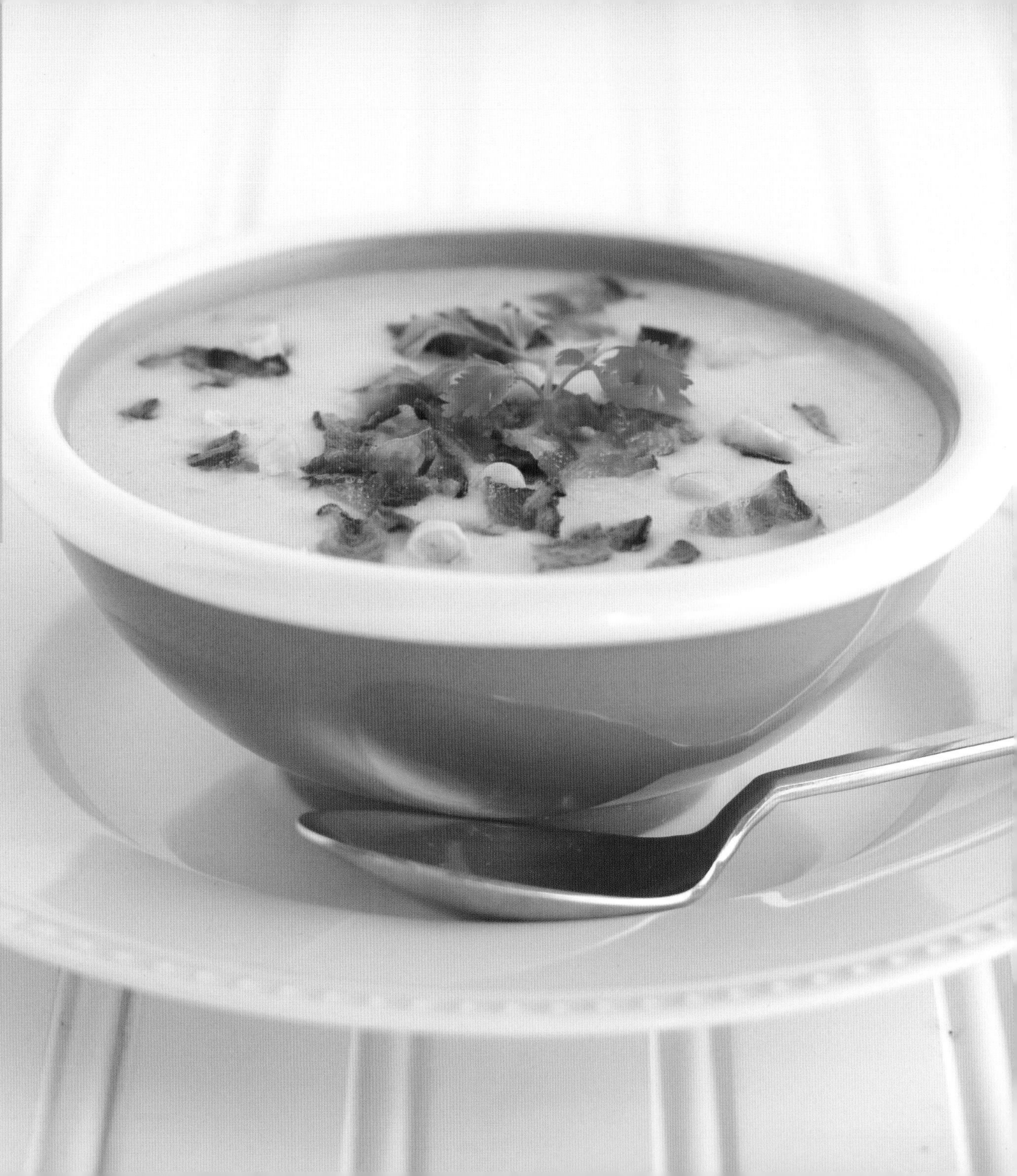

 **MAKES 6 TO 8 SERVINGS**

Jalapeño Corn Chowder

THE DISTINCTIVE KICK OF **JALAPEÑO PEPPERS** ENLIVENS THIS MILD CORN CHOWDER AND MAKES IT SPECIAL. SERVE WITH **CRISPY** WARM FLOUR **TORTILLAS**.

INGREDIENTS

4 slices bacon, chopped

1 yellow onion, chopped

2 jalapeño peppers, halved and seeded

2 cloves garlic, peeled, minced

¼ cup all-purpose white flour

6 cups chicken broth

2 russet potatoes, peeled and diced

½ tsp kosher salt

½ tsp ground black pepper

2 cups yellow corn kernels, uncooked

2 cups half and half cream

1 cup sharp cheddar cheese, shredded

2 tbsp fresh cilantro, minced

DIRECTIONS

In a large stockpot, cook bacon over medium-high heat until crisp. Remove bacon with a slotted spoon and set aside. Reduce heat to medium and add onion and peppers. Sauté, stirring frequently, until softened, about 8 to 10 minutes. Add garlic and cook for an additional minute. Whisk in flour and cook for 2 to 3 minutes, whisking constantly. Whisk in chicken broth, add potatoes, salt and pepper and bring to a boil. Reduce heat and simmer until potatoes are tender, about 12 minutes. Add corn and cream and simmer on low heat for 5 minutes, until corn is tender and heated through.

Ladle half of the soup into the blender and press Start. Gradually increase speed to medium and blend until smooth. Stir blended soup back into stockpot and adjust seasonings to taste. Heat briefly, if desired. Garnish each serving with bacon, cheese and cilantro.

Calories: 253 Fat: 15g; Chol: 46mg; Sodium: 108mg; Carb: 22g; Fiber: 2g; Protein: 10g

MAKES 4 TO 6 SERVINGS

Canadian Cheddar Cheese Soup

IF IT IS **SNOWING OUTSIDE**, IT IS TIME TO MAKE THIS SMOOTH, **COMFORT—FOOD** SOUP.

INGREDIENTS

1 tbsp olive oil

1 small onion, chopped

1 rib celery, chopped

2 cloves garlic, peeled and minced

2 tbsp butter, at room temperature

3 tbsp all-purpose white flour

¼ tsp dry mustard

1 tsp Worcestershire sauce

¼ tsp salt

½ tsp black pepper

1 cup whole milk

2 cups chicken stock

1¾ cups sharp cheddar cheese, shredded

½ cup dark hoppy bottled beer

DIRECTIONS

In a large stockpot, heat oil over medium heat. Add onion and celery and sauté until softened, about 6 to 8 minutes. Add garlic and sauté for an additional minute. Transfer vegetables to blender. Add butter, flour, mustard, Worcestershire sauce, salt, pepper, milk, chicken stock and cheese. Press Start and gradually increase speed to high until smooth, about 1 minute. Return soup to stockpot and simmer over low heat, whisking frequently until thickened. Add beer and whisk again until well-combined. Simmer 3 to 5 minutes until warm throughout. Do not allow soup to boil. Serve hot.

Calories: 253 Fat: 19g; Chol: 41mg; Sodium: 456mg; Carb: 7g; Fiber: 0g; Protein: 10g

Chicken Wrap with Artichoke Pesto, Spinach & Kalamat Olives, page 134

127

MAKES 2 SANDWICHES

Turkey, Manchego & Sun-dried Tomato Pesto Melt

FULLY LOADED WITH **FLAVOR**, THIS IS A SUBSTANTIAL **MEAL** TO BE EATEN OUT OF HAND.

INGREDIENTS

4 slices sourdough bread

2 tbsp butter, softened

2 tbsp Sun-dried Tomato Pesto (see recipe p. 182)

8 oz roasted turkey, thinly sliced

4 slices manchego cheese

DIRECTIONS

Spread one side of each bread slice with butter. Position 2 slices of bread, buttered side down, in a cold skillet and spread each with a generous amount of the pesto. Divide turkey and cheese equally on the pesto-cover slices and heat on medium. Spread the unbuttered side of the 2 remaining bread slices with pesto and place on top of the 2 sandwiches in the pan, buttered side up. Cook until bottom slices are golden brown, flip and continue cooking. Cook until bread is golden, turkey is heated through and cheese is melted. Slice on the diagonal and serve while hot.

Calories: 442 Fat: 23g; Chol: 68mg; Sodium: 1349mg; Carb: 28g; Fiber: 1g; Protein: 28g

MAKES 2 SERVINGS

Pork Tenderloin on Ciabatta Roll with Roasted Red Pepper Pesto

TART AND **SWEET PORK** TENDERLOIN IS PAIRED WITH **CRUNCHY SLAW** AND SLATHERED WITH RED PEPPER PESTO.

INGREDIENTS

1 tbsp apple cider vinegar

2 tbsp low fat mayonnaise

¼ tsp salt

¼ tsp black pepper

1¼ cups green cabbage, shredded

1 green onion, chopped

2 tbsp fresh parsley, chopped

¾ cup roasted red peppers

1 clove garlic, peeled

2 tbsp pine nuts

2 tbsp olive oil

¼ tsp Aleppo chile powder

2 ciabatta rolls, halved

4 oz roasted pork tenderloin, thinly sliced

DIRECTIONS

In a medium bowl, whisk together vinegar, mayonnaise, salt and pepper. Add cabbage, onion and parsley, tossing well to coat. Cover and chill.

Place red peppers, garlic, pine nuts and oil into blender and press Start. Pulse to coarsely chop. Add chile powder and gradually increase speed to medium. Blend until chunky-smooth. Spread cut side of each ciabatta half generously with red pepper pesto. Layer pork and slaw equally over the pesto and top with remaining ciabatta halves. Refrigerate any remaining pesto in an airtight container for up to 1 month.

Calories: 499 Fat: 32g; Chol: 134mg; Sodium: 975mg; Carb: 36g; Fiber: 3g; Protein: 31g

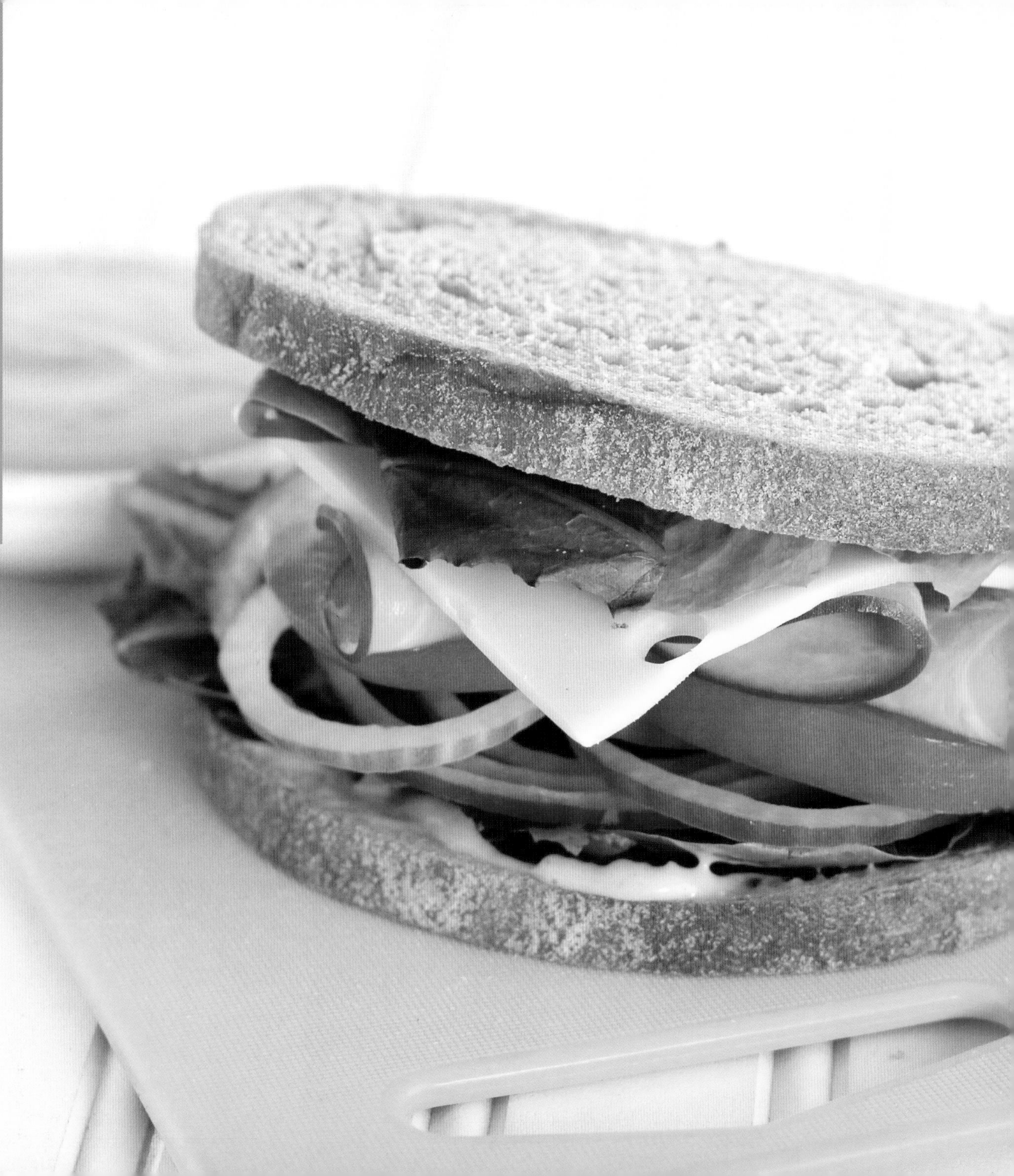

MAKES 2 SANDWICHES

Smoked Ham & Swiss with Honey Dijon Spread on Rye

A **SPICY DIJON** SPREAD TRANSFORMS PEDESTRIAN HAM AND SWISS INTO A **HEAVENLY** SANDWICH.

INGREDIENTS

1 cup mayonnaise (use lowfat, if desired)

1 shallot, peeled

2 tbsp Dijon mustard

1 tbsp honey

4 slices rye bread

8 oz smoked black forest ham, thinly sliced

4 slices low fat Swiss cheese

4 leaves red lettuce

red onion, thinly sliced

red tomato, sliced

DIRECTIONS

Place mayonnaise, shallot, mustard and honey into blender and press Start. Gradually increase speed to medium and blend until almost smooth. Spread mixture generously over each slice of bread. Layer 2 slices of bread with ham, cheese, lettuce, onion and tomato. Top with remaining slices of bread, cut diagonally and serve. Spoon any remaining spread into an air-tight container and refrigerate for up to one month.

Calories: 529 Fat: 15g; Chol: 60mg; Sodium: 3191mg; Carb: 61g; Fiber: 4g; Protein: 35g

MAKES 4 BURRITOS

California Garden Breakfast Burrito

A DELICIOUS **BURRITO-ON-THE-GO**; ADD CRISP **BACON BITS** OR CHOPPED COOKED TURKEY, CHICKEN OR HAM FOR A MEAL THAT WILL **GIVE YOU ENERGY** ALL DAY.

INGREDIENTS

2 tbsp water

6 eggs, at room temperature

¼ red bell pepper, seeded, cut in half

2 green onions, white and light green parts only, roughly chopped

3 tbsp fresh basil leaves

½ tsp salt

1 tsp ground black pepper

2 tbsp butter

4 small flour tortillas, warmed

½ red tomato, chopped

½ ripe avocado, chopped

½ cup prepared salsa, optional

DIRECTIONS

Place water in blender. Press Start and select low speed. Crack eggs one at a time and add separately through the lid opening. Increase speed to medium and continue blending until frothy. Add bell pepper, green onions, basil, salt and pepper and Pulse until chopped.

Heat a skillet over low heat and add butter when hot. When butter is melted, add egg mixture and scramble with a fork until set, but still slightly moist. Divide eggs evenly between tortillas and top each with tomato and avocado. Fold in the top and bottom of each tortilla about 1-inch, then tightly roll from one side to close. Serve with salsa, if desired.

Calories: 327 Fat: 41g; Chol: 278mg; Sodium: 969mg; Carb: 21g; Fiber: 3g; Protein: 13g

MAKES 2 SANDWICHES

BLT with Chipotle Spread

USE ANY EXTRA SPREAD ON **FLOUR TORTILLAS** AND TOP WITH A BIT OF **SHREDDED CHEESE**; BROIL FOR **3 MINUTES** AND CUT INTO WEDGES TO SERVE.

INGREDIENTS

½ cup low fat mayonnaise

1 canned chipotle pepper in adobo sauce

½ shallot, peeled

¼ tsp garlic powder

4 slices sourdough bread

6 slices bacon, cooked crisp

2 ripe tomatoes, sliced

6 leaves romaine lettuce

DIRECTIONS

Place mayonnaise, pepper and sauce, shallot and garlic powder into blender. Press Start and gradually increase speed to medium. Blend until well-combined. Toast bread lightly. Spread 1 side of each bread slice generously with chipotle mixture. Layer 2 slices of bread with bacon, tomato and lettuce and top with remaining slices of bread. Cut diagonally and serve. Refrigerate any remaining spread in an airtight container for up to 1 month.

Calories: 334 Fat: 16g; Chol: 28mg; Sodium: 1336mg; Carb: 36g; Fiber: 3g; Protein: 15g

MAKES 4 WRAPS

Chicken Wrap with Artichoke Pesto, Spinach & Kalamata Olives

A CREAMY **TOASTED WALNUT** AND ARTICHOKE SPREAD FORMS THE PERFECT **PARTNERSHIP** WITH CHICKEN AND SPINACH. **ALL WRAPPED UP** TO PERFECTION!

INGREDIENTS

4 small flour tortillas

¼ cup Artichoke Walnut Pesto (see recipe p. 185)

8 oz grilled chicken breast, thinly sliced

½ cup fresh spinach leaves

¼ cup kalamata olives, chopped

2 tbsp red onion, chopped

DIRECTIONS

Spread each wrap with pesto and layer with remaining ingredients. To wrap, fold over 1-inch top and bottom of each wrap, then tightly roll from one side to close. May be refrigerated overnight, wrapped tightly in plastic wrap.

Calories: 248 Fat: 11g; Chol: 50mg; Sodium: 913mg; Carb: 19g; Fiber: 1g; Protein: 18g

MAKES 2 SANDWICHES

Tri-tip and Arugula on Crusty French Rolls with Blue Cheese Apricot Spread

THE MARRIAGE OF **APRICOTS** AND BLUE CHEESE MAKES FOR ONE **HAPPY** TRI-TIP BEEF SANDWICH.

INGREDIENTS

2 oz low fat cream cheese

2 tbsp low fat mayonnaise

2 tbsp apricot preserves

2 oz blue cheese, crumbled

2 crusty French rolls, halved

4 oz cooked tri-tip beef, thinly sliced

¾ cup fresh arugula leaves

DIRECTIONS

Place cream cheese, mayonnaise and apricot preserves into blender and press Start. Gradually increase speed to high and blend until very smooth, scraping down sides as needed. Add blue cheese and Pulse once. Spread mixture generously over cut side of roll halves. Divide beef and arugula equally and top each with remaining half. Cut on the diagonal and serve. Refrigerate any remaining spread in an airtight container for up to 1 month.

Calories: 403 Fat: 17g; Chol: 58mg; Sodium: 828mg; Carb: 36g; Fiber: 1g; Protein: 26g

MAKES 4 TO 6 SERVINGS

Quick Sausage Breakfast Bake

THERE WILL BE NO **LATE SLEEPERS** WITH THIS LUSCIOUS BAKED EGG DISH ON THE **BREAKFAST** TABLE.

INGREDIENTS

2 cups lowfat milk

½ tsp salt

½ tsp ground black pepper

8 eggs, at room temperature

2 tbsp butter, at room temperature

4 to 6 slices sourdough bread

½ lb bulk sweet Italian sausage, cooked and crumbled

¼ cup fresh Italian parsley, chopped

2 cups mozzarella cheese, shredded

DIRECTIONS

Preheat oven to 350°F. Place milk, salt and pepper into blender and press Start. With speed on low, blend the mixture and add the eggs, one at a time, through the lid opening. Blend on medium speed until frothy.

Lightly butter an oven-proof 9 x 9-inch baking pan and line bottom with bread slices. Cover bread with crumbled sausage and carefully pour egg mixture over all. Sprinkle parsley over eggs and top with mozzarella cheese. Bake for 35 to 40 minutes, until eggs are firm in center and top is lightly browned. Cool slightly and cut into squares.

Calories: 385 Fat: 24g; Chol: 285mg; Sodium: 976mg; Carb: 14g; Fiber: 2g; Protein: 24g

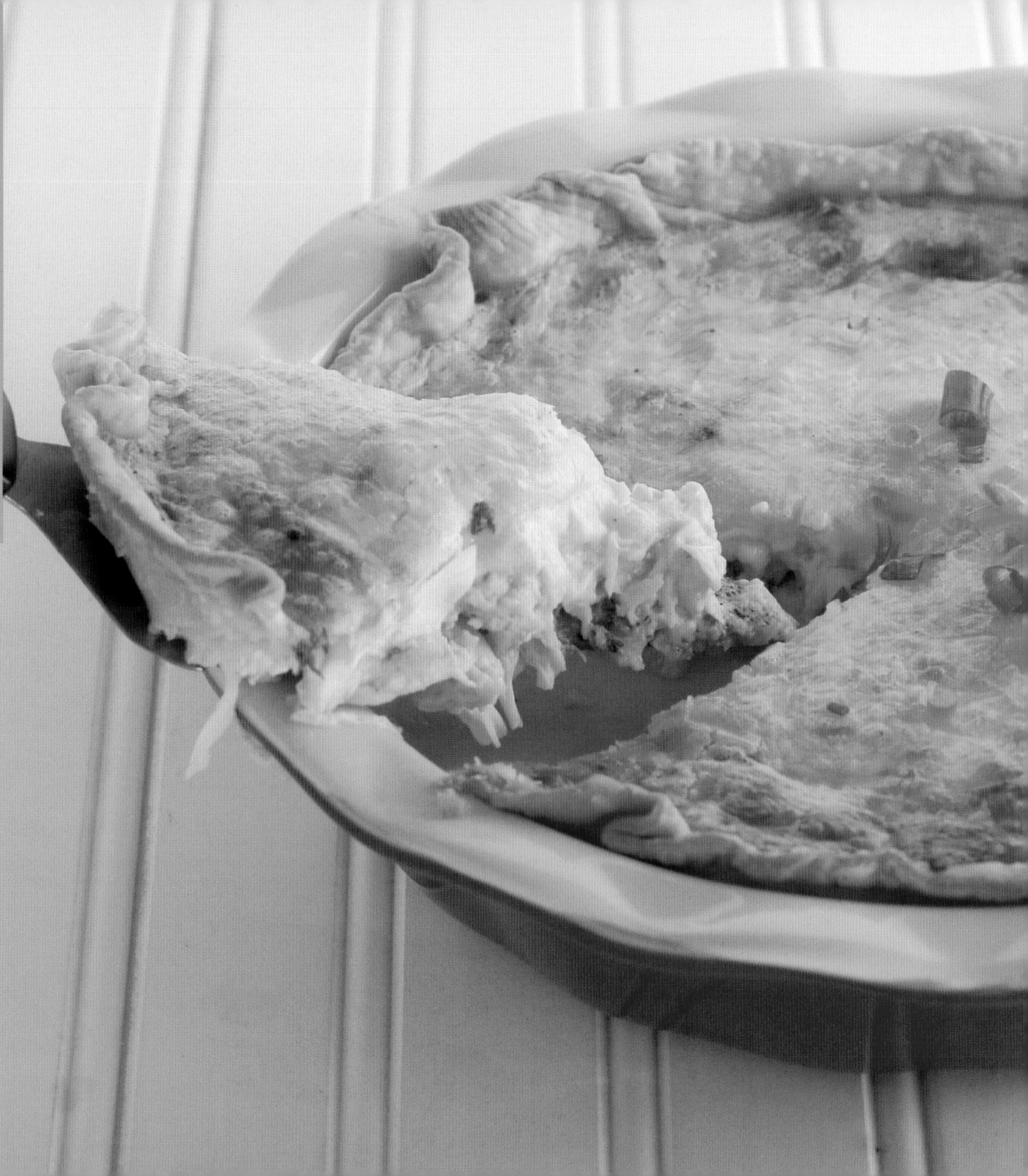

MAKES 6 TO 8 SERVINGS

Herbed Crab Quiche

THE JAMBA PROFESSIONAL BLENDER MAKES **SHORT WORK** OF THIS DELICATE QUICHE. **ENJOY**!

INGREDIENTS

1 tbsp olive oil

2 green onions, white and light green parts only, chopped

½ lb fresh asparagus, roughly cut

1 prepared pie crust, rolled out and arranged in 9-inch pie plate

1½ cups whole milk

1 tbsp whole-grain mustard

½ tsp salt

½ tsp black pepper

½ tsp Old Bay® seafood seasoning

⅛ tsp ground nutmeg

4 eggs, at room temperature

6 oz fresh lump crab meat

1½ cups gruyere cheese, grated

DIRECTIONS

Preheat oven to 350°F. Heat oil in a sauté pan over medium-high heat. Add green onions and asparagus and sauté until tender, about 4 to 5 minutes. Cool slightly and arrange evenly over bottom of pie crust. Place milk, mustard, salt, pepper, seafood seasoning and nutmeg into blender and press Start. Gradually increase speed to medium. With blender running, add eggs, one at a time, through the lid opening and continue blending on medium speed until smooth.

Pour egg mixture over vegetables and evenly cover with crab and cheese. Bake for 50 to 60 minutes, or until quiche is set in the center and lightly golden on top. Cool slightly before serving.

Calories: 274 Fat: 17g; Chol: 141mg; Sodium: 464mg; Carb: 16g; Fiber: 1g; Protein: 16g

cook's note:

TO PREVENT PASTRY *edges* FROM BAKING TOO QUICKLY, COVER EDGES *with foil* STRIPS WHEN LIGHTLY BROWNED.

MAKES 4 SERVINGS

Fettuccine with Artichoke Alfredo Sauce

FOR **SPECIAL OCCASIONS**, THIS CREAMY, SAUCE-LADEN PASTA ANSWERS THE CALL **PERFECTLY**.

INGREDIENTS

½ cup low fat milk

½ cup half and half

½ cup canned artichoke hearts in water, drained

2 tbsp all-purpose white flour

¼ tsp garlic powder

½ cup Parmesan cheese, grated

pinch salt

¼ tsp ground black pepper

1 lb fettuccine pasta, cooked and drained

DIRECTIONS

Place all ingredients, except fettuccine, into blender. Press Start and gradually increase speed to medium-low. Blend until smooth. Transfer to a small saucepan and cook over low heat, whisking constantly, for 3 to 5 minutes, until sauce has thickened. Toss sauce with cooked fettuccine and serve hot.

Calories: 548 Fat: 19g; Chol: 23mg; Sodium: 318mg; Carb: 92g; Fiber: 4g; Protein: 24g

MAKES 8 SERVINGS

Beef Tenderloin with Blender Horseradish Chive Sauce

BEEF TENDERLOIN IS **MILD IN FLAVOR**; THIS SAUCE WAKES IT UP **DELICIOUSLY**.

INGREDIENTS

2½ lb beef tenderloin roast, trimmed

1 tbsp olive oil

½ tsp salt

1 tsp ground black pepper

¼ cup Blender Fresh Horseradish (see recipe p. 184)

1 cup lowfat sour cream

¼ tsp salt

¼ tsp ground black pepper

2 tbsp chives, chopped

DIRECTIONS

Preheat the oven to 400 F. Rub roast with oil and season with salt and pepper. Place roast in a large oven-safe skillet over medium high heat and sear on all sides, about 4 to 6 minutes. Place skillet in preheated oven and roast for about 25 to 30 minutes, or until the internal temperature reaches 135°F for rare or 150°F for medium. Loosely cover with foil and let rest for 10 minutes.

While tenderloin is cooking, place horseradish, sour cream, remaining salt and pepper into blender and press Start. Gradually increase speed to medium until smooth, scraping down sides as needed. Add chives and Pulse once or twice to combine. Slice tenderloin in thin strips and serve with Horseradish Chive Sauce.

Calories: 249 Fat: 11g; Chol: 69mg; Sodium: 305mg; Carb: 2g; Fiber: 0g; Protein: 33g

Poached Salmon with Dill Cucumber Yogurt Sauce

SALMON **COOKS VERY QUICKLY**, WHICH MAKES IT A GREAT CHOICE FOR A DELICIOUS MID-WEEK MEAL. THE TRICK FOR **PERFECTLY PREPARED** SALMON IS TO COOK IT FOR 10 MINUTES PER INCH OF THICKNESS AND YOU WILL HAVE A **WINNER** EVERY TIME.

INGREDIENTS

4 1-inch thick salmon filets

1 lemon, juiced

2 tbsp olive oil

1 tsp salt

1 tsp ground black pepper

1 cup white wine

1 cup water

2 cups plain Greek yogurt

½ cucumber, peeled, roughly cut

4 tsp fresh dill, chopped, divided

1 tsp fresh marjoram, chopped (optional)

½ tsp salt

½ tsp ground black pepper

DIRECTIONS

Preheat oven to 400°F. Place salmon in a large oven-proof baking pan and drizzle lemon juice evenly over the filets. Drizzle with oil and sprinkle with one teaspoon each salt and pepper. Place baking pan in oven, add wine and water and poach for 10 minutes. While salmon is poaching, place yogurt, cucumber, 2 teaspoons dill, marjoram, if using, and remaining salt and pepper into blender and press Start. Gradually increase speed to medium and blend until smooth. When salmon is done, remove from oven, cool slightly and serve topped with yogurt sauce and garnished with remaining dill.

Calories: 308; Fat: 15g; Chol: 44mg; Sodium: 694mg; Carb: 8g; Fiber: 0g; Protein: 20g

MAKES 6 TO 8 SERVINGS

Brussels Sprouts with Herb Butter Sauce

LITTLE **CABBAGES** ARE GETTING A LOT OF **ATTENTION** THESE DAYS. THE SAUCE OFFERED HERE WILL ADD TO THE ENTICINGLY **TENDER** BRUSSELS SPROUTS.

INGREDIENTS

2 lbs Brussels sprouts, trimmed and halved

½ lemon, cut into pieces

¾ cup butter, melted

1 tbsp walnut oil or olive oil

2 tbsp fresh parsley, chopped

2 tbsp fresh marjoram, chopped

2 tbsp fresh thyme, chopped

¼ tsp salt

½ tsp ground white pepper

DIRECTIONS

Place lemon into water in steamer pan, place steamer basket over water and add Brussels sprouts. Steam sprouts 6 to 10 minutes, to desired doneness. Place butter, oil, parsley, marjoram, thyme, salt and pepper into blender and press Start. Pulse until well-combined. Transfer steamed Brussels sprouts to serving bowl and drizzle with herbed butter sauce. Serve while hot.

Calories: 209 Fat: 19g; Chol: 45mg; Sodium: 291mg; Carb: 8g; Fiber: 3g; Protein: 3g

Roasted Lemon Garlic Potatoes

SERVE WITH **SIMPLE** BAKED CHICKEN FOR A **MEMORABLE** MEAL.

INGREDIENTS

8 cloves garlic, peeled and crushed

½ cup olive oil

2 lemons, juiced

2 tbsp fresh rosemary

1 tsp salt

1 tsp ground black pepper

4 russet potatoes, peeled and cut into wedges

½ cup chicken broth

DIRECTIONS

Preheat oven to 400°F. Press Start and, with the blender running at low speed, drop the garlic into the blender through the lid opening to finely chop. Stop the blender and add olive oil, lemon juice, rosemary, salt and pepper. Press Start, gradually increase speed to medium and blend until smooth.

In a large bowl, toss potatoes with garlic lemon mixture and arrange in an oven-proof 9 x 13-inch baking pan. Cover pan tightly with foil and bake for 15 minutes. Remove foil, add chicken broth and continue baking for an additional 25 to 30 minutes, or until potatoes are tender and cooked through with crispy edges. For crispier potatoes, switch oven heat to broiler and broil potatoes until golden brown, about 3 to 4 minutes.

Calories: 281 Fat: 18g; Chol: 0mg; Sodium: 446mg; Carb: 28g; Fiber: 2g; Protein: 4g

MAKES 4 TO 6 SERVINGS

Kale & Quinoa Salad

THIS **SUBSTANTIAL SALAD** CAN BE A
STAND-IN FOR A MEATLESS **MAIN DISH** OR HEARTY LUNCHEON ENTREE.

INGREDIENTS

2 cloves garlic, peeled and crushed

⅓ cup olive oil

¼ cup apple cider vinegar

1 lemon, juiced

2 tbsp tahini (sesame seed paste)

½ tsp salt

¼ tsp ground cumin

2 cups quinoa, cooked, kept hot

2 cups fresh kale, finely shredded

2 tbsp pine nuts, toasted

2 tbsp dried cranberries

DIRECTIONS

Press Start and add the garlic to the blender through the lid opening. Gradually increase the speed to medium and finely chop the garlic. Add the oil, vinegar, lemon juice, tahini, salt and cumin and continue blending until smooth.

In a serving bowl, combine hot quinoa with kale, pine nuts and cranberries. Add sesame dressing, tossing well to combine. Serve hot, warm or chilled.

Calories: 267 Fat: 19g; Chol: 0mg; Sodium: 208mg; Carb: 26g; Fiber: 4g; Protein: 30g

MAKES 6 TO 8 SERVINGS

Asparagus with Curry Cream Sauce

JUST A HINT OF **CURRY** AWAKENS THESE **DELICATE** ASPARAGUS SPEARS.

INGREDIENTS

½ cup butter, melted

½ cup white wine

4 hard-cooked egg yolks

½ cup silken tofu

3 tbsp lemon juice

2 tsp curry powder

1 tsp salt

4 cloves garlic, smashed

2 lbs thin asparagus spears

DIRECTIONS

Place all ingredients, except garlic and asparagus, into blender and press Start. Gradually increase speed to medium and blend until very smooth, adding additional wine if needed. Set aside.

Place garlic cloves into water in steamer pan, place steamer basket over water and add asparagus. Steam asparagus 3 to 4 minutes until tender-crisp and arrange in a serving dish. Drizzle curry cream sauce over the asparagus and serve while hot.

Consuming raw or undercooked meats, poultry, seafood, shellfish, or eggs may increase your risk of foodborne illness.

Calories: 169 Fat: 14g; Chol: 135mg; Sodium: 401mg; Carb: 5g; Fiber: 2g; Protein: 5g

MAKES 14 SLICES

Nutty Pumpkin Loaf

PACKED WITH **WHOLESOME** INGREDIENTS, THIS BREAD IS BEST WHEN SERVED WARM. SERVE WITH **CREAM CHEESE** OR **CRÈME FRAICHE** FOR A **SPECIAL TREAT**.

INGREDIENTS

¼ cup butter, melted

2 eggs

¼ cup vegetable oil

1 cup granulated sugar

½ cup lowfat milk

1 cup pumpkin purée (not pumpkin pie filling)

1 tsp pure vanilla extract

1 cup whole wheat flour

1 cup all-purpose white flour

1 tsp baking soda

1 tsp ground pumpkin pie spice

½ tsp ground ginger

½ tsp salt

½ cup dried apricots, chopped

½ cup pecans, chopped

DIRECTIONS

Preheat oven to 350°F. Lightly coat a 9-inch loaf pan with cooking spray. Set aside.

Place butter, eggs, oil and sugar into blender and press Start. Gradually increase speed to medium and blend until smooth. Add milk, pumpkin and vanilla and blend again on medium until well-combined. In a large mixing bowl, combine flours, soda, spices and salt. Scrape blender mixture into dry ingredients, stirring until just incorporated. Fold in apricots and pecans and stir by hand.

Spoon batter into the pan and bake for 50 to 60 minutes, until a pick inserted into the center comes out clean. Slice and serve while warm.

Calories: 216 Fat: 8g; Chol: 35mg; Sodium: 184mg; Carb: 33g; Fiber: 3g; Protein: 4g

MAKES 12 MUFFINS

Blackberry Bran Muffins

SUBSTITUTE **BOYSENBERRIES** OR BLUEBERRIES
IN THESE **WHOLESOME** MUFFINS.

INGREDIENTS

1 egg, at room temperature

1 cup lowfat milk

¼ cup canola oil

¾ cup brown sugar, packed

1 cup whole wheat flour

1 cup oat bran

1 tbsp flax seeds

2 tsp baking powder

½ tsp baking soda

½ tsp ground cinnamon

½ tsp kosher salt

1 cup fresh blackberries

DIRECTIONS

Preheat oven to 375°F. Lightly coat a 12-cup muffin pan or line with paper baking cups. Place egg, milk, oil and brown sugar into blender and press Start. Gradually increase speed to medium and blend to combine.

In a large mixing bowl, combine flour, oat bran, flax seeds, baking powder, soda, cinnamon and salt. Add blender ingredients to dry ingredients and stir by hand just until combined. Fold in blackberries and spoon batter into prepared muffin cups, filling each about three-fourths full. Bake for 15 to 20 minutes or until tops are golden brown and a pick inserted into center comes out clean. Serve warm.

Calories: 171 Fat: 6g; Chol: 16mg; Sodium: 118mg; Carb: 29g; Fiber: 3g; Protein: 4g

Sweet Balsamic Strawberry Ricotta Muffins

A DELICIOUSLY **GOURMET** MUFFIN!

INGREDIENTS

1½ cups strawberries, halved

1 tbsp brown sugar

1 tbsp balsamic vinegar

2 eggs, at room temperature

¾ cup lowfat milk

½ cup canola oil

1 cup granulated sugar

1 tsp pure vanilla extract

2 cups all-purpose white flour

2 tsp baking powder

¼ tsp baking soda

½ tsp salt

½ cup ricotta cheese

DIRECTIONS

In a medium glass bowl, toss strawberries, brown sugar and balsamic vinegar and marinate at room temperature for 1 hour. Drain juices and set aside.

Preheat oven to 375°F. Lightly coat a 12-cup muffin pan with cooking spray or line with paper baking cups. Prepare a 6-cup muffin pan in the same manner. Set aside.

Place eggs, milk, oil, sugar and vanilla into blender and press Start. Gradually increase speed to medium to blend until combined. In a large mixing bowl, combine flour, baking powder, soda and salt. Spoon the liquid ingredients into the dry ingredients and combine. Fold in ricotta cheese and strawberries, stirring until just incorporated. Spoon batter into prepared muffin cups, filling each about three-fourths full. Bake for 15 to 20 minutes or until tops are golden brown and a toothpick inserted into center comes out clean. Serve warm.

Calories: 176 Fat: 8g; Chol: 25mg; Sodium: 83mg; Carb: 24g; Fiber: 1g; Protein: 3g

MAKES 12 TO 14 PINWHEELS

Caraway Parmesan Pinwheels

A LOVELY **ACCOMPANIMENT** TO HOT SOUP OR A **CHILLED SALAD.**

INGREDIENTS

1 cup water, warmed to 110-115°F

¼ oz pkg active dry yeast

1 tsp sugar

3 tbsp olive oil, divided

2¼ cups all-purpose white flour, divided

1 tsp salt

1 tsp caraway seeds

½ cup Parmesan cheese, grated

½ tsp freshly ground black pepper

oil to coat bowl and spatula

DIRECTIONS

Place water, yeast, sugar and two tablespoons oil into blender and set aside for 5 minutes. When foamy, press Start and Pulse to blend for 10 seconds. Combine 1 cup flour with salt and add to blender. Pulse to incorporate. Add remaining flour in one-fourth cup increments, Pulsing after each addition to form a sticky dough.

With an oiled spatula, transfer dough to a lightly oiled bowl and turn to coat all sides. Cover with a clean towel and let rise until doubled in size, about 30 to 45 minutes. Line a large baking sheet with parchment paper and set aside.

Preheat oven to 350°F. Pat dough into a rectangle one-half inch thick. Brush with remaining oil and sprinkle with caraway seeds, cheese and pepper. Roll up tightly, starting on the short side and cut into one-inch pinwheels. Place pinwheels, cut side down, on prepared baking sheet. Cover loosely with a cloth and let rise until doubled in size, about one hour. Bake for 10 to 15 minutes. Serve while warm.

Calories: 115 Fat: 4g; Chol: 3mg; Sodium: 238mg; Carb: 16g; Fiber: 1g; Protein:3g

Carrot Cake with Ginger Cream Frosting, page 160

MAKES 2 SERVINGS

Mocha Frappe Milkshake

THE ADDITION OF OATS AND **PROTEIN POWDER** **ELEVATE** THIS MILKSHAKE TO A POWERHOUSE.

INGREDIENTS

2 cups frozen lowfat chocolate ice milk

½ cup regular or quick-cooking oats, uncooked (do not use instant oatmeal)

1 cup brewed coffee, chilled

2 scoops chocolate protein powder

1 tsp pure vanilla extract

8 to 10 ice cubes

DIRECTIONS

Place all ingredients into blender in the order listed and press Start. Gradually increase speed and blend on medium until smooth. Divide between glasses and serve immediately.

Calories: 355 Fat: 8g; Chol: 65mg; Sodium: 100mg; Carb: 40g; Fiber: 4g; Protein: 29g

 **MAKES 2 SERVINGS**

Mango Cardamom Milkshake

TRADITIONAL **THAI DRINKS** OFTEN COMBINE MANGO AND CARDAMOM. THE FLAVORS MELD WELL WITH **COCONUT MILK** HERE, AS WELL.

INGREDIENTS

1½ cups light coconut milk

2 tbsp organic honey

1 large ripe mango, peeled, pitted, cut in chunks

1 tsp ground cardamom

6 to 8 ice cubes

whipped cream for garnish

caramel sauce for garnish

DIRECTIONS

Place all ingredients into blender, except the garnishes, and press Start. Gradually increase the speed and blend on high speed until smooth. Divide evenly between two tall glasses, top with whipped cream and a drizzle of caramel. Serve at once.

Calories: 262 Fat: 13g; Chol: 0mg; Sodium: 38mg; Carb: 37g; Fiber: 2g; Protein: 1g

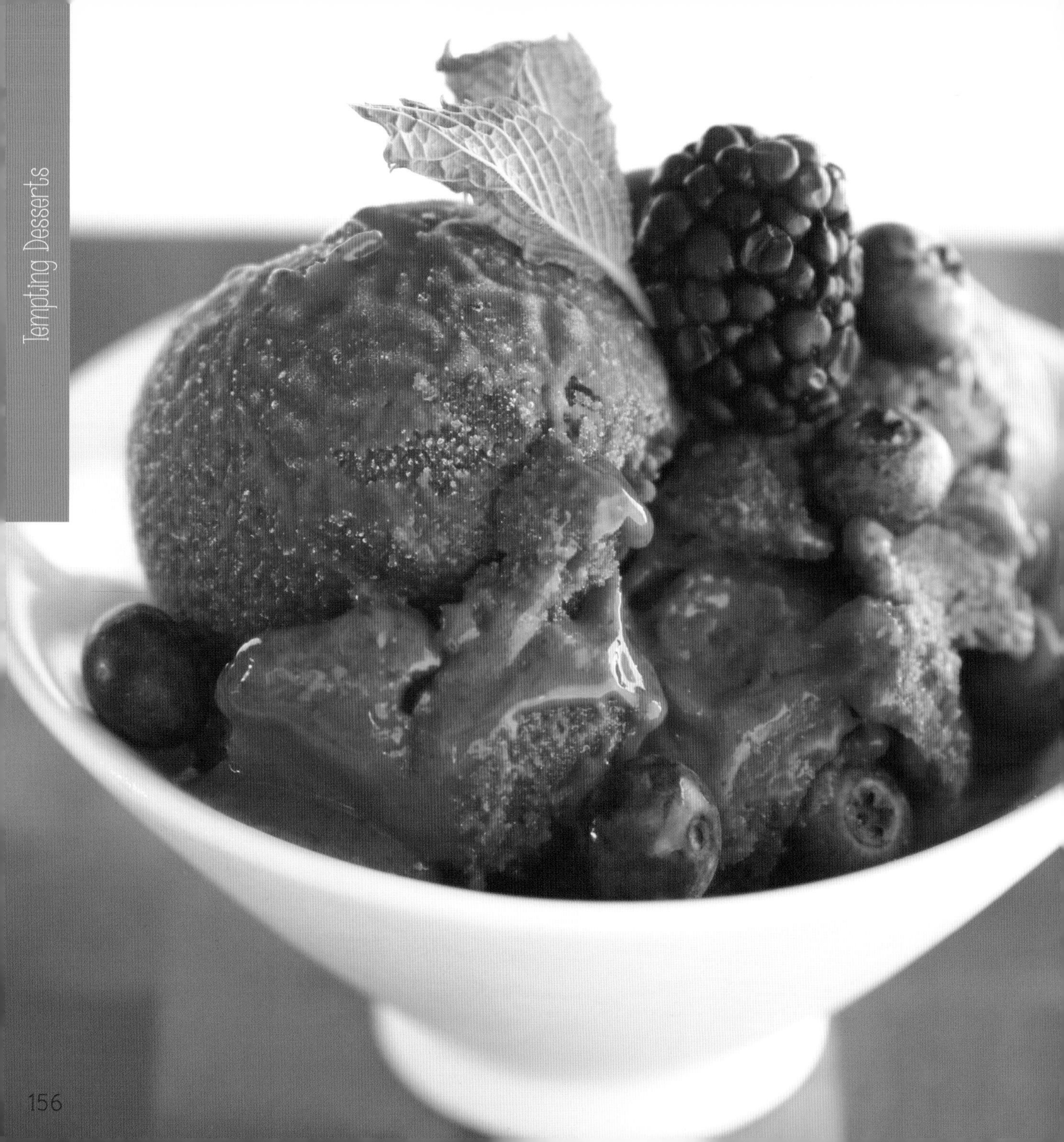

MAKES ABOUT 6 TO 8 SERVINGS

Black & Blueberry Frozen Yogurt

BERRIES ARE THE JEWELS THAT MAKE A **FROZEN TREAT** REALLY **SHINE**.

INGREDIENTS

1 cup fresh blackberries

1½ cups fresh blueberries

½ cup organic honey

2 tbsp lime juice

pinch salt

2 cups plain yogurt (do not use lowfat or nonfat yogurt)

fresh berries for garnish

fresh mint for garnish

DIRECTIONS

In a medium saucepan over medium heat, combine berries, honey, lime juice and salt and simmer for 10 minutes, stirring to combine. Cool mixture completely and transfer to blender. Press Start and gradually increase speed to high. Blend until very smooth. To remove seeds, press mixture through fine sieve into a large bowl. Add the yogurt, mixing well to thoroughly combine. Cover and refrigerate for several hours or overnight until thoroughly chilled. Transfer mixture to ice cream maker and follow manufacturer's instructions. Serve garnished with berries and mint.

Calories: 136 Fat: 3g; Chol: 8mg; Sodium: 92mg; Carb: 26g; Fiber: 2g; Protein: 6g

MAKES 4 TO 6 SERVINGS

Dark Chocolate Gelato

DECADENT AND **RICH**, DARK CHOCOLATE GELATO IS **BEST** WHEN SERVED IN SMALL CUPS.

INGREDIENTS

2 egg yolks

2 tbsp dark cocoa powder

¼ cup granulated sugar

½ tsp pure vanilla extract

pinch salt

1 cup whole milk, divided

1 cup heavy cream

2 oz dark chocolate, roughly chopped

DIRECTIONS

Start the blender and gradually increase speed to medium high. Drop the egg yolks, one at a time, into blender through the lid opening and blend until frothy. Stop blender and add cocoa powder, sugar, vanilla, salt and one-half cup milk in order listed. Replace lid and press Start. Gradually increase speed to high until mixture is well-blended.

Heat remaining milk and heavy cream in a medium saucepan over low heat until bubbles form around edge of pan. With blender running on medium speed, slowly pour scalded milk through the lid opening and blend until smooth. Return mixture to saucepan and simmer over medium heat, stirring frequently until mixture thickens. Strain through a fine mesh sieve.

Cover and refrigerate for several hours or overnight until thoroughly chilled. Stir in chocolate, transfer mixture to ice cream maker and freeze according to manufacturer's instructions.

Calories: 272 Fat: 22g; Chol: 129mg; Sodium: 46mg; Carb: 17g; Fiber: 2g; Protein: 4g

 **MAKES 4 SERVINGS**

Cherry Banana Sorbet

LIGHT AND **FRUITY** SORBET, MADE IN JUST **MINUTES**!

INGREDIENTS

1 cup vanilla almond milk

1 tsp pure vanilla extract

2 frozen bananas, peeled, cut in half

2 cups frozen cherries, pitted

banana slices for garnish

chopped sweet cherries for garnish

DIRECTIONS

Place milk, extract and frozen fruit into blender in order listed. Press Start and gradually increase speed to high and blend until smooth. Garnish each serving with bananas and cherries and serve at once.

Calories: 166 Fat: 3g; Chol: 0mg; Sodium: 38mg; Carb: 39; Fiber: 6g; Protein: 2g

cook's note:

SUBSTITUTE *low-fat* SOY, RICE, HEMP OR COW'S MILK, IF DESIRED.

MAKES 12 TO 16 SERVINGS

Carrot Cake with Ginger Cream Frosting (Gluten Free)

SURPRISE YOUR **GLUTEN-FREE** FRIENDS WITH LUSCIOUS CARROT CAKE!

INGREDIENTS

CAKE:

4 carrots, roughly chopped

1¼ cups vegetable oil

3 eggs

½ cup granulated sugar

1 cup brown sugar, packed

1½ tsp pure vanilla extract

2 cups Gluten Free Flour (see recipe p. 208)

2 tsp ground cinnamon

1 tsp baking soda

1 tsp salt

½ tsp ground ginger

½ tsp ground cardamom

½ cup raisins

½ cup pecans, chopped

FROSTING:

8 oz cream cheese, at room temperature

¼ cup unsalted butter

2 tsp pure vanilla extract

3 cups powdered sugar

1-2 tbsp heavy cream

¼ cup crystalized ginger, chopped

crystalized ginger for garnish (optional)

pecan halves for garnish, optional

DIRECTIONS

Preheat oven to 350°F. Grease two 9-inch cake rounds. Line with parchment paper, grease and flour parchment. Place carrots and oil into blender and press Start. Pulse on a medium speed until carrots are finely chopped. Add eggs, sugars and vanilla and blend for 1 minute. In a large bowl, whisk flour, cinnamon, soda, salt, ginger and cardamom.

Spoon blender mixture into into dry ingredients. Add raisins and pecans. Stir well. Divide batter between prepared pans and bake until tops are golden brown and pick inserted into center comes out clean, about 25 to 30 minutes. Cool for 15 minutes. Invert layers and cool on rack.

To make frosting, place the cream cheese, butter and vanilla in the blender and press Start. Blend on medium until whipped. Stop and add the sugar. Blend on medium, adding cream through lid opening, until frosting is smooth. Add ginger by hand. Place one layer on serving plate and frost top generously. Center remaining layer on top. Frost sides, then top and garnish with optional ginger and pecans. Refrigerate for 30 minutes to set before serving.

Calories: 471 Fat: 31g; Chol: 59mg; Sodium: 234mg; Carb: 43g; Fiber: 1g; Protein: 3g

MAKES 4 SERVINGS

Grilled Pineapple with Mango Lime Sauce

PINEAPPLE IS SO **NATURALLY SWEET** AND GRILLING JUST BRINGS OUT EVEN MORE **DEPTH** OF FLAVOR.

INGREDIENTS

4 large slices pineapple, about 1-inch thick

1 tbsp coconut oil

1 ripe mango, peeled, pitted, cut into chunks

3 tbsp organic honey

3 tbsp lime juice

pinch ground red chile

pinch salt

DIRECTIONS

Brush pineapple slices with oil and grill over medium-high heat, 2 to 4 minutes per side. Place remaining ingredients into blender and process until smooth. Serve grilled pineapple slices drizzled with mango lime sauce.

Calories: 130 Fat: 4g; Chol: 0mg; Sodium: 54mg; Carb: 27g; Fiber: 2g; Protein: 1g

cook's note:
TO SERVE AS A REFRESHING APPETIZER, *garnish* WITH CHOPPED *avocado* AND DICED RED ONION.

Honey Walnut & Black Pepper Cookies

EVERY CULTURE HAS A VERSION OF THESE **CELEBRATORY COOKIES** THAT GRACE THE TABLES AT **WEDDINGS** AND **HOLIDAYS**. THIS RECIPE BORROWS BITS FROM **SPAIN**, **ITALY** AND **GREECE** TO CREATE A DELICATE COOKIE **PERFECT** FOR YOUR SPECIAL OCCASIONS.

INGREDIENTS

1¾ cups walnuts, shelled, divided

1 cup unsalted butter, at room temperature

¼ cup granulated sugar

¼ cup honey

¾ tsp ground black pepper

¼ tsp salt

2 cups all-purpose white flour

¾ cup powdered sugar

DIRECTIONS

Coarsely chop one-half cup walnuts and set aside. Place remaining walnuts into blender and press Start. Pulse until most walnuts are finely ground. Add butter, granulated sugar, honey, pepper and salt and blend on low speed until well-combined, scraping down sides as needed. Place flour and chopped walnuts into a large bowl, stir in mixture from blender, and mix well to form dough. Wrap dough in plastic wrap and refrigerate until chilled, at least 30 minutes.

Preheat oven to 300°F. Line baking sheets with parchment paper and set aside. Roll heaping teaspoons of dough into small balls, place on the baking sheet and flatten slightly with the tines of a fork. Bake for 15 to 18 minutes or until bottoms are golden brown. Remove from oven and sprinkle immediately with powdered sugar. Cool slightly and transfer to a rack to cool completely. Store in an airtight container for up to 3 days.

Calories: 180 Fat: 13g; Chol: 20mg; Sodium: 78mg; Carb: 2g; Fiber: 1g; Protein: 2g

Tempting Desserts

MAKES 8 TO 12 CREPES

Raspberry Ricotta Crêpes

LIGHT AND **DELICATE**, THESE CRÊPES ARE THE PERFECT **COMPLEMENT** TO THE RASPBERRIES AND **RICOTTA** CHEESE.

INGREDIENTS

1 cup all-purpose white flour

1 tsp granulated sugar

¼ tsp salt

2 eggs, at room temperature

1¼ cups lowfat milk

3 tbsp butter, melted

1 cup ricotta cheese

2 tbsp powdered sugar

3 cups fresh raspberries

2 tsp butter, plus additional for cooking

DIRECTIONS

Place flour, granulated sugar, salt, eggs, milk and 3 tablespoons butter into blender and press Start. Blend on medium speed until smooth. Cover and refrigerate for one hour.

Melt 2 teaspoons butter in a nonstick skillet over medium heat. Add one-fourth cup batter and swirl pan to coat bottom evenly. Cook crêpe until underside is lightly golden, about 1 to 2 minutes. Flip crêpe and cook for an additional minute. Slide crêpe from pan and keep warm while repeating process with remaining batter. Add butter as needed to coat the pan.

In a small bowl, combine ricotta with powdered sugar. Cover half of each crêpe with ricotta cheese and fold crêpe over into quarters. Top with berries and serve.

Calories: 136 Fat: 7g; Chol: 20mg; Sodium: 123mg; Carb: 14g; Fiber: 14g; Protein: 6g

MAKES 4 SERVINGS

Mocha Chia Coconut Pudding

A BRIGHT MORNING TREAT TOPPED WITH A **DOLLOP OF WHIPPED CREAM**, FRESH FRUIT AND **TOASTED** NUTS.

INGREDIENTS

2 cups coconut milk

6 tbsp chia seeds

2 tsp instant coffee

1 tsp cocoa powder

1 tsp granulated sugar

whipped cream for garnish

ripe berries for garnish

toasted slivered almonds for garnish

DIRECTIONS

Place milk, seeds, instant coffee, cocoa powder and sugar into blender and press Start. Blend on medium speed until thoroughly blended. Pour into medium bowl and let set for 5 minutes. Stir by hand every 5 minutes until mixture begins to thicken. Refrigerate until pudding reaches desired thickness. Serve with a dollop of whipped cream, a spoonful of berries and a few slivered almonds.

Calories: 127 Fat: 10g; Chol: 0mg; Sodium: 25mg; Carb: 6g; Fiber: 3g; Protein: 1g

MAKES 8 SERVINGS

Dark Chocolate Chess Pie

DESSERT IS A **ONE-STEP PROCESS** FOR THIS
PIE! THE **CHOCOLATE** PIE **COMES TOGETHER** QUICKLY INSIDE THE
JAMBA® PROFESSIONAL BLENDER.

INGREDIENTS

½ cup butter, melted

1½ cups granulated sugar

¼ cup dark cocoa powder

1 tbsp all-purpose white flour

¼ tsp salt

1 tsp pure vanilla extract

2 eggs, at room temperature

15 oz can evaporated milk

9-inch pie crust, unbaked

2 cups whipped cream for garnish

DIRECTIONS

Preheat oven to 350°F. Place melted butter into blender and add sugar, cocoa powder, flour, salt, vanilla, eggs and evaporated milk. Press Start and gradually increase speed to medium, blending until mixture is smooth. Pour into unbaked pie crust and bake for 40 to 50 minutes, until pie is set and pick inserted into center comes out clean. Cool completely. Garnish with whipped cream before serving.

Calories: 431 Fat: 21g; Chol: 79mg; Sodium: 355mg; Carb: 57g; Fiber: 1g; Protein: 8g

MAKES 8 POPS

Kiwi Coconut Frozen Pops

THE **CHIA SEEDS** TUCKED INSIDE THESE FROZEN POPS CREATE A LITTLE BIT OF **TEXTURE** AND **INTEREST**.

INGREDIENTS

1¾ cups lowfat coconut milk

1½ cups fresh kiwi, cut in chunks

3 tbsp agave nectar

1 cup shredded unsweetened coconut

1 tbsp chia seeds

DIRECTIONS

Place coconut milk, kiwi and agave into blender and press Start. Gradually increase speed to high and blend until very smooth. Add coconut and chia seeds and Pulse once to combine. Fill 8 frozen pop molds three-fourths full and freeze until solid. Serve frozen.

Calories: 151 Fat: 11g; Chol: 0mg; Sodium: 15mg; Carb: 15g; Fiber: 3g; Protein: 1g

MAKES 8 POPS

Raspberry Orange Frozen Fruit Pops

FOR CHILDREN, FOR THE **NEIGHBOR NEXT DOOR**, FOR THE BABYSITTER, OR FOR ANYONE WHO LIKES A **SIMPLE TREAT**.

INGREDIENTS

2 cups frozen raspberries

2 large oranges peeled, seeded

1 lime, juiced

½ cup water

DIRECTIONS

Place all ingredients into blender and press Start. Gradually increase speed to high and blend until very smooth. Fill 8 frozen pop molds about three-fourths full and freeze until solid. Serve frozen.

Calories: 146 Fat: 2g; Chol: 0mg; Sodium: 3mg; Carb: 64g; Fiber: 19g; Protein: 6g

cook's note:

KIDS LOVE TO MAKE THEIR OWN POP **molds** WITH PAPER CUPS AND **wooden sticks**!

Chocolate, Almond & Peanut Cups

DISCLAIMER—MUCH LIKE THE **WELL-KNOWN** PEANUT BUTTER CUP CANDIES, THESE **FROZEN TREATS** ARE ADDICTIVE!

INGREDIENTS

1½ cups blanched almonds

¼ cup regular or quick-cooking oats, uncooked (do not use instant oatmeal)

½ cup creamy or crunchy peanut butter

3 tbsp coconut oil

½ cup powdered sugar

¼ tsp salt

1 cup dark chocolate chips

DIRECTIONS

Line 12-cup or 24-mini cup muffin pan with paper baking cups. Set aside.

Place almonds, oats, peanut butter and coconut oil into blender and press Start. Blend on a low speed, gradually increasing to a medium speed. Blend for about 10 seconds, reduce speed to low and blend until combined. Scrape down sides of blender as needed. Add sugar and salt and blend to a chunky-smooth texture.

Divide dough equally between the prepared muffin cups, pressing dough firmly into each cup to create an even layer. Place chocolate chips in a glass measuring cup and microwave on 50% power in 45 second increments until melted. Spoon chocolate over the nut cups, dividing evenly among all. Freeze until chocolate is firm, about 40 to 45 minutes. Serve frozen or store in freezer in an airtight container for up to 1 month.

Calories: 146 Fat: 11g; Chol: 0mg; Sodium: 51mg; Carb: 12g; Fiber: 2g; Protein: 4g

Maple Vanilla Bean Frozen Pops

A FROZEN POP, COMPLETE WITH **INTENSE VANILLA FLAVOR**, OFFERING SOPHISTICATED SATISFACTION.

INGREDIENTS

1 cup sweetened vanilla almond milk

2 cups lowfat vanilla ice cream

1 cup lowfat vanilla-flavored yogurt

3 tbsp pure maple syrup

1 fresh vanilla bean, split

DIRECTIONS

Place almond milk, ice cream, yogurt and maple syrup into blender. Slit the vanilla bean lengthwise and scrape paste into blender. Press Start and gradually increase speed to high. Blend until mixture is smooth. Fill 8 frozen pop molds three-fourths full and freeze until solid. Serve frozen.

Calories: 47 Fat: 1g; Chol: 0mg; Sodium: 41mg; Carb: 10g; Fiber: 0g; Protein: 2g

Chapter 9

Signature Sauces & Marinades

Fresh Tomato Basil Sauce, page 188

MAKES ABOUT 2 CUPS

Maple Mustard Whiskey Marinade

PERFECTLY **SUITED** TO BEEF OR PORK.

INGREDIENTS

¾ cup whiskey

¼ cup olive oil

¼ cup maple syrup

1 shallot, peeled, cut in half

¼ small fennel bulb, trimmed

1 tbsp Dijon mustard

1 tsp salt

1 tsp ground black pepper

DIRECTIONS

Place all ingredients into blender and press Start. Gradually increase speed to high and blend until smooth. Use at once or refrigerate in an airtight container for up to 2 weeks.

Calories: 33 Fat: 2g; Chol: 0mg; Sodium: 80mg; Carb: 2g; Fiber: 0g; Protein: 0g

MAKES ABOUT 2³/₄ CUPS

Italian Roasted Garlic & Red Wine Marinade

ALTHOUGH THE MARINADE WORKS WELL WITH
CUTS OF BEEF AND PORK, IT IS ALSO DELICIOUS AS A **ROOT VEGETABLE**
MARINADE. **GRILL MARINATED VEGETABLES** FOR SUPERIOR RESULTS.

INGREDIENTS

2 cups red wine

¼ cup olive oil

¼ red onion, peeled

8 cloves garlic, roasted, peeled

1 tbsp dried basil

1 tbsp dried thyme

1 tsp salt

1 tsp ground black pepper

DIRECTIONS

Place all ingredients into blender and press Start. Gradually increase speed to high and blend until smooth. Use at once or refrigerate in an airtight container for up to 2 weeks.

Calories: 25 Fat: 2g; Chol: 0mg; Sodium: 71mg; Carb: 0g; Fiber: 0g; Protein: 0g

MAKES ABOUT 1¹/₂ CUPS

Simple Chipotle Marinade

CHILES AND **ONION** FORM THE BASE OF **ZESTY MARINADES** AND SAUCES. THIS MARINADE WORKS WELL WITH **BEEF**, **CHICKEN** OR CUTS OF **PORK**.

INGREDIENTS

3 cloves garlic, peeled

3 canned chipotle chilies, with ¼ cup adobo sauce

½ onion, peeled

¼ cup honey

¼ cup canola oil

3 tbsp apple cider vinegar

2 tbsp tomato paste

1 tsp ground black pepper

1½ tsp ground cumin

DIRECTIONS

Press Start and, with blender running on low speed, drop the garlic cloves through the lid opening to finely chop. Stop blender and add all remaining ingredients. Press Start and gradually increase speed to high. Blend until smooth. Use at once or refrigerate in an airtight container for up to 2 weeks.

Calories: 45 Fat: 3g; Chol: 0mg; Sodium: 148mg; Carb: 5g; Fiber: 0g; Protein: 0g

MAKES ABOUT 2¼ CUPS

Quick & Easy No-Cook Applesauce

VERSATILE AND **WELL-LOVED**, THIS APPLESAUCE CAN BE SERVED AS IS, ADDED TO **CAKE BATTER** OR USED AS WONDER**FULLY NATURAL** TODDLER FOOD. THE FLAVOR NEVER DISAPPOINTS.

INGREDIENTS

¼ cup unfiltered apple juice

2 tbsp honey

4 apples, peeled, cored, roughly cut

¾ tsp ground cinnamon

dash nutmeg

DIRECTIONS

Place all ingredients into blender in order listed and press Start. Gradually increase speed to medium and blend until chunky-smooth. Use at once or refrigerate in an airtight container for up to 10 days.

To make applesauce for babies or toddlers, blend the apple mixture until very smooth. Divide into single-use portions, pack into airtight containers and refrigerate for up to 10 days. After serving, discard any remaining applesauce. Freeze applesauce in airtight single-use portions for up to 1 month. Thaw before serving and discard any remaining applesauce after serving.

Calories: 112 Fat: 0g; Chol: 0mg; Sodium: 3mg; Carb: 29g; Fiber: 4g; Protein: 0g

MAKES ABOUT 1¹/₂ CUPS

Red Chile Almond Sauce

TRY THIS OVER **GRILLED FISH** IN A LA

ROMESCO-FASHION. DELICIOUS!

INGREDIENTS

1 large dried red chile, stem and seeds removed

³/₄ cup water

1 tbsp + 1 tsp olive oil, divided

¹/₄ yellow onion, peeled

¹/₃ cup blanched almonds, toasted

¹/₄ tsp ground cumin

¹/₄ tsp dried oregano

¹/₂ tsp salt

2 tsp lime juice

³/₄ cup chicken stock

DIRECTIONS

Break chile into pieces and place into blender with water. Press Start and Pulse a few times to crumble. Let stand in blender for 1 hour (to soften chile). In a medium sauté pan, heat one teaspoon oil over medium-high heat. Add onion and sauté until softened, about 6 to 8 minutes. Set aside.

Add the sautéed onion and remaining ingredients to the chile-water mixture in the blender. Press Start and gradually increase speed to high. Blend for 5 minutes until very smooth. Use right away or refrigerate in an airtight container for up to 1 week.

Calories: 38 Fat: 4g; Chol: 0mg; Sodium: 1319mg; Carb: 1g; Fiber: 0g; Protein: 1g

MAKES ABOUT 2¹/₂ CUPS

No-Cook Blender Mexican Verde Sauce

POURED OVER **GRILLED CHICKEN** OR SPOONED INTO A **BEAN AND RICE BURRITO**, THIS **VERDE SAUCE** ADDS THE KICK TO EVERY DISH IT ADORNS.

INGREDIENTS

¾ cup water

1 tbsp lime juice

4 sprigs cilantro, trimmed

¼ yellow onion, peeled

1 clove garlic, peeled

1 small jalapeño pepper, seeded, roughly cut

½ tsp salt

8 tomatillos, husked, washed and halved

DIRECTIONS

Place all ingredients into blender and press Start. Gradually increase speed to high and blend until mixture is chunky-smooth. Let stand to allow flavors to marry for 1 hour. Use at once or refrigerate in an airtight container for up to 3 days.

Calories: 4 Fat: 0g; Chol: 0mg; Sodium: 48mg; Carb: 1g; Fiber: 0g; Protein: 0g

cook's note:

FOR A NUTRITIONAL BOOST, ADD 1 CUP *fresh kale* OR SPINACH LEAVES BEFORE BLENDING.

MAKES ABOUT 2¹/₂ CUPS

Dairy-Free Red Pepper Cream Sauce

INCREDIBLE FLAVOR IN A **DAIRY-FREE** CREAM SAUCE!
ADD THE **SMOKED PAPRIKA** TO AMP UP THE IMPRESSION.

INGREDIENTS

1 tbsp olive oil

½ yellow onion, chopped

2 cloves garlic, peeled and minced

3 red peppers, cored, seeded and roasted

¼ cup pine nuts, toasted

¾ cup unsweetened hemp or almond milk

½ tsp salt

¼ tsp smoked paprika, optional

DIRECTIONS

Heat oil in a medium sauté pan over medium-high heat. Add onion and sauté until softened, about 6 to 8 minutes, stirring often. Add garlic and sauté for one minute. Transfer onion mixture to blender and add all remaining ingredients. Press Start and gradually increase speed to high, blending for about 5 minutes until sauce is very smooth. Use right away or refrigerate in an airtight container for up to 2 days.

Calories: 18 Fat: 1g; Chol: 0mg; Sodium: 5mg; Carb: 1g; Fiber: 0g; Protein: 0g

 **MAKES ABOUT 3 CUPS**

Creamy Cauliflower Sauce

A LUSCIOUS AND **SILKY-SMOOTH** ALTERNATIVE TO HIGH-FAT SAUCES. SPOON OVER PRIMAVERA **VEGETABLES** OR COOKED **WHOLE GRAINS**.

INGREDIENTS

½ cup whole milk

2 tsp fresh lemon juice

½ large head cauliflower, trimmed and steamed

1 tbsp butter, softened

2 cloves garlic, peeled

½ tsp salt

½ tsp freshly ground black pepper

DIRECTIONS

Place all ingredients in the order listed into the blender and press Start. Gradually increase speed to high and blend 5 minutes until smooth. Add a few tablespoons milk if a thinner sauce is desired. Use right away or refrigerate in an airtight container for up to 2 days.

Calories: 11 Fat: 1g; Chol: 1mg; Sodium: 54mg; Carb: 1g; Fiber: 0; Protein: 0g

MAKES 2 CUPS

Sun-dried Tomato Pesto

A RICH **FULL-BODIED PESTO**, PERFECT FOR SPOONING ON **FLATBREAD** OR TOSSING INTO WARM PASTA.

INGREDIENTS

2 8.5 oz jars sun-dried tomatoes, packed in olive oil

6 cloves garlic, peeled

1 tsp salt

2 tsp ground black pepper

2 cups fresh basil leaves, loosely packed

1 cup Parmesan cheese, freshly grated

DIRECTIONS

Place tomatoes with oil, garlic, salt and pepper in the blender and press Start. Pulse until coarsely chopped. Add the basil and cheese and blend on medium-high until smooth. Use as your recipe directs or refrigerate in an airtight container for up to 1 month.

Calories: 42 Fat: 3g; Chol: 2mg; Sodium: 149mg; Carb: 3g; Fiber: 1g; Protein: 2g

MAKES ABOUT 1½ CUPS

Cilantro Piñon Pesto

USE AS A **DRESSING** FOR SALADS OR
SPOON OVER FILLED, **HOT TACOS**.

INGREDIENTS

2 cups fresh cilantro leaves, loosely
packed

2 cloves garlic, peeled

¼ cup pine nuts, toasted

½ cup Parmesan cheese, grated

1 tbsp lemon juice

¼ tsp salt

¼ tsp ground black pepper

½ cup olive oil

DIRECTIONS

Place cilantro, garlic, pine nuts, cheese, juice, salt and pepper into
blender. Press Start and gradually increase speed to medium. Pulse
and use tamper to roughly chop, scraping down sides as needed. With
blender running, gradually drizzle oil through the lid opening, blending
on low speed and slowly increasing to medium-high speed until the
pesto is desired consistency. Use at once or refrigerate in an airtight
container for up to 5 days.

Calories: 58 Fat: 6g; Chol: 2mg; Sodium: 78mg; Carb: 0g; Fiber: 0g; Protein: 1g

MAKES ABOUT 12 OUNCES

Blender Fresh Horseradish

SHARPLY FLAVORFUL AND A PERFECT **WAKE-UP CALL** TO CUTS OF BEEF.

INGREDIENTS

¼ cup water

½ cup white wine vinegar

4 oz horseradish root, peeled, roughly cut

⅛ tsp salt

DIRECTIONS

Place all ingredients into blender and press Start. Gradually increase speed to high and blend until smooth. Use right away or refrigerate in an airtight glass jar for up to 6 weeks.

Calories: 4 Fat: 0g; Chol: 0mg; Sodium: 21mg; Carb: 1g; Fiber: 0g; Protein: 0g

MAKES 1¹/₂ CUPS

Artichoke Walnut Pesto

THIS PESTO **COMES TOGETHER** QUICKLY WITH THE ADDITION OF **ARTICHOKE** HEARTS **PACKED** IN OIL. USE IN SANDWICHES, PASTA SALADS OR **DRIZZLED** OVER GRILLED BEEF.

INGREDIENTS

2 6 oz jars marinated artichoke hearts in olive oil

¹/₂ cup walnuts, toasted

¹/₂ cup fresh parsley, loosely packed

4 cloves garlic, peeled

1 tsp salt

1 tsp ground black pepper

2 tbsp olive oil

DIRECTIONS

Place the artichoke hearts with the oil, walnuts and parsley in the blender and press Start. Pulse until coarsely chopped. Add the garlic, salt, pepper and olive oil and blend on medium until smooth. Use as your recipe directs or refrigerate in an airtight container for up to 1 month.

Calories: 15 Fat: 1g; Chol: 0mg; Sodium: 128mg; Carb: 0g; Fiber: 0g; Protein: 0g

MAKES ABOUT 1¹/₂ CUPS

Gremolata

TRADITIONALLY SERVED WITH **VEAL**, THIS IS ALSO EXCELLENT WHEN SPOONED ONTO **GRILLED** OR BAKED FISH.

INGREDIENTS

1 cup fresh parsley leaves, loosely packed

1 cup fresh basil leaves, loosely packed

1 clove garlic, peeled

¹/₂ shallot, peeled

¹/₄ tsp salt

¹/₄ tsp ground black pepper

¹/₄ cup olive oil

2 tbsp lemon peel

DIRECTIONS

Place parsley, basil, garlic, shallot, salt and pepper in the blender and press Start. Gradually increase speed to medium and blend until roughly chopped, scraping down sides of blender if needed. Add oil and lemon peel and Pulse 2 to 4 times to combine. Serve chilled or at room temperature. Use right away or refrigerate for up to 2 days.

Calories: 41 Fat: 5g; Chol: 0mg; Sodium: 46mg; Carb: 0g; Fiber: 0g; Protein: 0g

MAKES 2 CUPS

Lebanese Garlic Sauce

LIBERALLY SPOON OVER **LAMB** FOR AN **EXOTIC** ENTRÉE ACCENT.

INGREDIENTS

8 cloves garlic, peeled

½ cup canned white beans, rinsed and drained

¼ cup lemon juice

½ tsp salt

1 cup sunflower oil

1 to 3 tbsp water

DIRECTIONS

With blender running on medium-high speed, drop the garlic through the lid opening to finely chop. Scrape down sides and add beans, lemon juice and salt. Press Start and Pulse a few times. With blender running on medium speed, slowly drizzle oil through the lid opening to form a sauce. When fully incorporated, drizzle in water, 1 tablespoon at a time, to create a smooth sauce. Use right away or refrigerate in an airtight container for up to 2 days.

Calories: 130 Fat: 14g; Chol: 0mg; Sodium: 73mg; Carb: 2g; Fiber: 0g; Protein: 1g

MAKES ABOUT 4¹/₂ CUPS

Fresh Tomato Basil Sauce

TOSSED OVER HOT PASTA, SPOONED INTO AN **OMELET**, OR SPREAD ON **ARTISAN BREAD**, THIS SAUCE IS BOTH FRESH AND **ZESTY**.

INGREDIENTS

½ cup olive oil

6 ripe tomatoes, cored, quartered

2 cloves garlic, peeled

½ tsp salt

½ tsp ground black pepper

¾ cup fresh basil leaves, packed

DIRECTIONS

Place oil, tomatoes, garlic, salt and pepper into blender and press Start. Gradually increase speed and blend on high until smooth. Add basil leaves and Pulse to chop and combine. Use at once or refrigerate in an airtight container for up to 2 days.

Calories: 61 Fat: 6g; Chol: 0mg; Sodium: 67mg; Carb: 2g; Fiber: 1g; Protein: 0g

 **MAKES 2 CUPS**

Blender White Sauce

A GOOD WHITE SAUCE RECIPE IS A **MUST-HAVE** IN ANY COOK'S REPERTOIRE. USE AS A **BASE** FOR CHEESE SOUPS, SCALLOPED POTATOES, MACARONI AND CHEESE OR CHICKEN POT PIE. ADD FRESHLY **GRATED NUTMEG** TO CREATE A LOVELY B CHAMÉL.

INGREDIENTS

¼ cup butter, at room temperature

1½ cups whole milk

¼ cup + 2 tsp all-purpose white flour

¼ tsp salt

DIRECTIONS

Place all ingredients into blender in the order listed. Press Start and blend on low speed, gradually increasing to high speed. Blend until sauce is completely incorporated and smooth. Transfer to a small saucepan and heat over low heat, whisking constantly until sauce is thickened. Use as your recipe directs. Refrigerate unused sauce in an airtight container for up to 2 days.

Calories: 46 Fat: 4g; Chol: 10mg; Sodium: 64mg; Carb: 3g; Fiber: 0g; Protein: 1g

MAKES ABOUT 3 CUPS

Texas Barbecue Sauce

THIS IS A **SERIOUS** TEXAS BBQ SAUCE;
CRAFTED TO **PERFECTION**.

INGREDIENTS

14.5 oz can whole San Marzano
tomatoes, with juice

½ white onion, peeled

2 cloves garlic, peeled

1 cup ketchup

⅔ cup apple cider vinegar

⅓ cup brown sugar, packed

2 tbsp tomato paste

2 tbsp Dijon mustard

1 tbsp Worcestershire sauce

2 tsp ground pepper

1 tsp ground cumin

1 tsp salt

DIRECTIONS

Place all ingredients into blender and press Start. Gradually increase speed to medium and blend until smooth. Taste and adjust seasoning, if needed. Transfer to a large saucepan and heat over medium-high heat, stirring often until boiling. Reduce heat to low and simmer, stirring frequently, for 1 hour. Taste and adjust seasoning. Use right away or cool and refrigerate in an airtight container for up to 2 weeks.

Calories: 18 Fat: 0g; Chol: 0mg; Sodium: 29mg; Carb: 4g; Fiber: 0g; Protein: 1g

MAKES ABOUT 2¹/₂ CUPS

Easy Blender Cheese Sauce

USE THIS QUICK CHEESE SAUCE SPOONED OVER **VEGETABLES**, EGGS, PASTA OR **OPEN–FACE** SANDWICHES.

INGREDIENTS

¼ cup butter, at room temperature

1½ cups whole milk

¼ cup + 2 tsp all-purpose white flour

½ tsp salt

¼ tsp ground white pepper

1 cup cheddar cheese, grated

DIRECTIONS

Place butter, milk, flour, salt and pepper into blender in the order listed. Press Start and gradually increase speed to high, blending until incorporated. Add cheese and Pulse a few times to blend. Transfer to a medium saucepan and heat over low heat, whisking constantly, until sauce is thickened. Use as your recipe directs. Refrigerate any unused sauce in an airtight container for up to 2 days.

Calories: 85 Fat: 7g; Chol: 20mg; Sodium: 165; Carb: 3g; Fiber: 0g; Protein: 3g

MAKES ABOUT 1¹/₂ CUPS

Easy Parsley Pesto

A **LIGHT TAKE** ON PESTO, THIS RECIPE
RELIES ON GARDEN PARSLEY TO **BOOST** THE **GARLICKY** FLAVOR.

INGREDIENTS

2 cups fresh parsley leaves, loosely packed

2 cloves garlic, peeled

¼ cup walnuts, toasted

½ cup Parmesan cheese, grated

2 tbsp lemon juice

¼ tsp salt

½ cup olive oil

DIRECTIONS

Place parsley, garlic, walnuts, cheese, lemon juice and salt into blender. Press Start and gradually increase speed to medium. Blend to a rough chop. Gradually drizzle oil into the blender through the lid opening and continue blending until smooth. Use at once or refrigerate in an airtight container for up to 5 days.

Calories 58 Fat 6g; Chol: 2mg; Sodium: 53mg; Carb: 0g; Fiber: 0g; Protein: 1g

Oat Flour,
page 21

MAKES 4 CUPS

Almond Milk

SOFTENING NUTS BY **SOAKING** MAKES THEM EASIER TO **DIGEST**.

INGREDIENTS

1 cup raw almonds

3 cups water, divided

1 cup ice cubes

DIRECTIONS

Soak almonds in enough water to cover for eight hours or overnight. Drain and discard water.

Place almonds into blender and add 2 cups water. Press Start and gradually increase speed to medium. Blend until almonds are coarsely chopped. Add remaining 1 cup water and ice and blend on high until very smooth. Strain through a cheesecloth-lined sieve and refrigerate in an airtight container for up to 5 days.

Calories: 156 Fat: 1g; Chol: 0mg; Sodium: 0mg; Carb: 5g; Fiber: 3g; Protein: 6g

• Sweeten or flavor almond milk by adding 1 teaspoon or more of vanilla extract, chocolate syrup, honey or agave nectar.

MAKES ABOUT 3 CUPS

Vanilla Soy Milk

DELICIOUS, FRESH FLAVOR WITHOUT **LACTOSE**.

INGREDIENTS

1 cup dried soybeans, picked though and rinsed

5 cups water

¼ cup agave nectar

2 tbsp pure vanilla extract

DIRECTIONS

Soak soybeans in enough water to cover for 10 hours or overnight. Drain water and discard.

Place soybeans into blender, add water and press Start. Gradually increase speed to high and blend for 4 minutes. Cool and strain through a cheesecloth-lined sieve. Transfer milk to a saucepan and bring to a boil, reduce heat and simmer for 15 minutes. Add agave and vanilla; simmer for 5 minutes. Cool and refrigerate in an airtight container for up to 5 days.

Calories: 364 Fat: 12g; Chol: 0mg; Sodium: 2mg; Carb: 41g; Fiber: 5g; Protein: 23g

SERVES 6 TO 8

Rice Milk Horchata

STRAIGHT FROM **MEXICO**, HORCHATA CALLS ON A SWEET **CINNAMON** FLAVOR TO APPEAL TO ALL AGES.

INGREDIENTS

1 cup long grain white rice, uncooked

2 cinnamon sticks, broken into pieces

1 vanilla bean, split

6 cups water, divided

¾ cup sweetened condensed milk

ice cubes

ground cinnamon for garnish, optional

DIRECTIONS

Place rice, cinnamon sticks, vanilla bean paste and 2 cups water into blender and press Start. Gradually increase speed to high and blend until coarsely chopped. Add 4 cups water and Pulse to incorporate. With lid on, set blender aside and soak for four hours. Add condensed milk to mixture and press Start. Gradually increase speed to high and blend until smooth. Strain in batches through a cheesecloth-lined sieve. Transfer to an airtight pitcher and chill until serving.

To serve, stir horchata well and pour into tall, ice-filled glasses. Garnish with a dash of ground cinnamon, if desired. Refrigerate horchata for up to 2 days.

Calories: 130 Fat: 1g; Chol: 2mg; Sodium: 18mg; Carb: 3g; Fiber: 0g; Protein: 3g

MAKES 2¼ CUPS

Gingerbread Apple Spread

FRESH AND FLAVORFUL, THIS APPLE SPREAD IS FABULOUS ADDED TO SMOOTHIES, SMEARED ON BAGELS OR SPOONED OVER VANILLA ICE CREAM.

INGREDIENTS

¼ cup unfiltered apple juice

2 tbsp maple syrup

4 large baking apples, peeled, cored and quartered

½ cup dark brown sugar, packed

1 tsp ground cinnamon

¼ tsp ground ginger

pinch ground nutmeg

pinch ground cloves

DIRECTIONS

Preheat oven to 275°F. Place all ingredients into blender and press Start. Gradually increase speed to medium-high and blend until smooth, scraping down sides as needed. Spoon into a 9 x 9-inch oven-proof baking pan and bake, uncovered, for 2 to 2½ hours. Stir every 30 minutes. When done, the sauce will be thick and glossy. Cool and use right away or refrigerate in airtight pint jars for up to 2 weeks.

Calories: 46 Fat: 0g; Chol: 0mg; Sodium: 2mg; Carb: 12g; Fiber: 1g; Protein: 0g

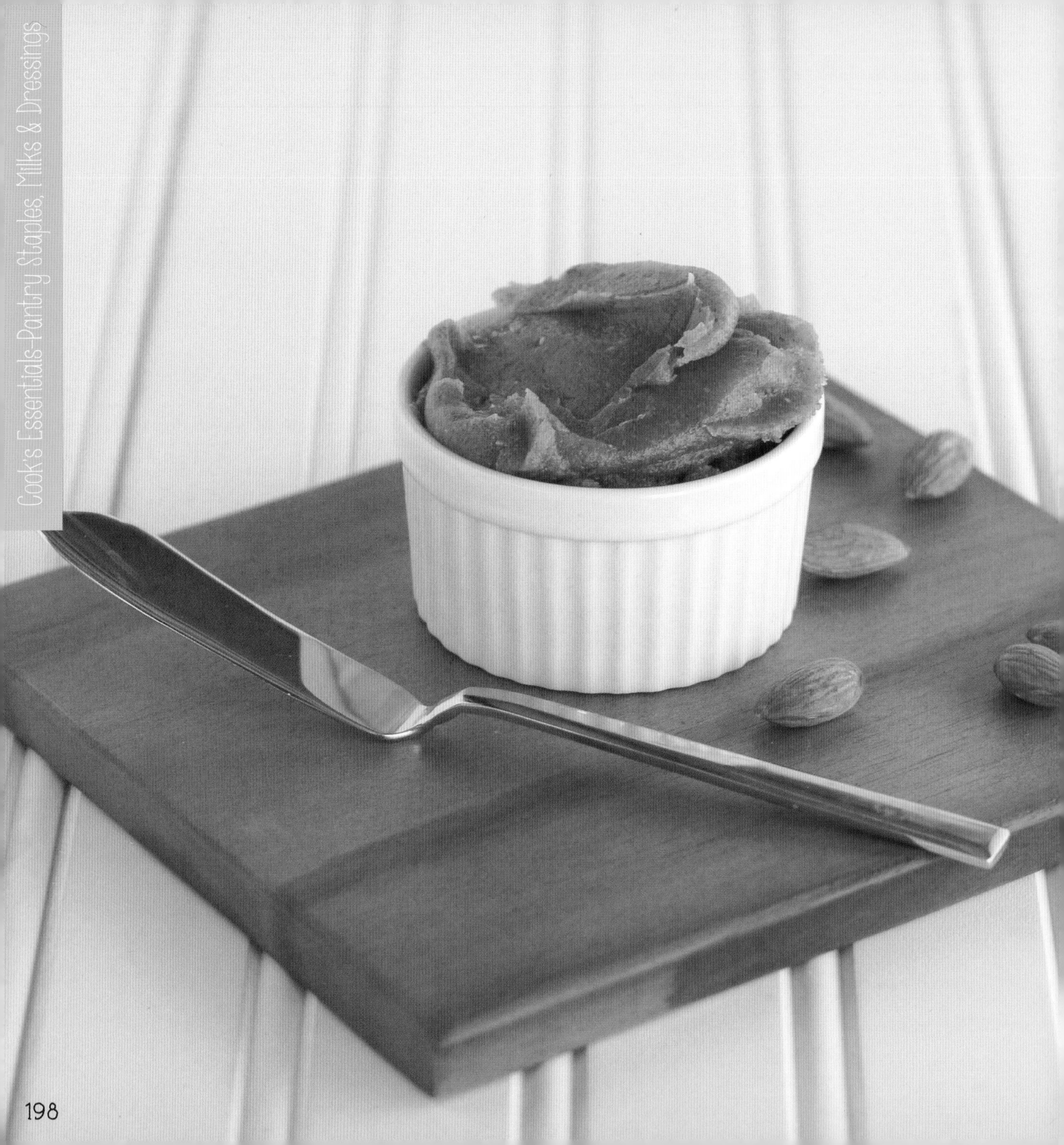

MAKES ABOUT 1¼ CUPS

Maple Almond Butter

USE ON WHOLE-GRAIN **PANCAKES**, WAFFLES OR TOAST. TRY IT ON BAKED **SWEET POTATOES** OR WITH STEAMED **BRUSSELS SPROUTS**. IF YOU ARE A **PURIST**, LICK IT OFF THE SPOON.

INGREDIENTS

2 cups roasted almonds

2 tbsp pure maple syrup

pinch salt

2 to 4 tbsp canola oil, optional

DIRECTIONS

Place almonds, syrup and salt into blender in order listed. Add oil, if using. Press Start and gradually increase speed to medium-high speed, blending until the mixture is chunky-smooth or as smooth as desired. Scrape down sides as needed. Transfer to an airtight container and refrigerate for up to 1 month.

Calories: 88 Fat: 7g; Chol: 0mg; Sodium: 11mg; Carb: 4g; Fiber: 2g; Protein: 3g

Herbed Lemon Butter

EXCELLENT **MELTED OVER** GRILLED SALMON OR A **BAKED POTATO**.

INGREDIENTS

1½ cups butter, melted

zest of 1 lemon

¼ cup fresh parsley leaves, loosely packed

2 tbsp fresh oregano

2 tbsp thyme leaves

DIRECTIONS

Place all ingredients into blender and press Start. Pulse 2 to 3 times until well-combined. Pour herbed butter into a container or butter molds and cover tightly. Refrigerate several hours or overnight. Use as desired. Refrigerate for up to 1 month.

Calories: 123 Fat: 14g; Chol: 37mg; Sodium: 98mg; Carb: 0g; Fiber: 0g; Protein: 0g

MAKES ABOUT 1 CUP

Cashew Butter

CASHEWS MAKE THE MOST RICH, LUSCIOUS BUTTER DUE TO THE HIGH FAT CONTENT OF THE NUTS. DON'T LET THIS SCARE YOU AWAY; IT ONLY TAKES A BIT TO ADD INTENSITY TO YOUR FAVORITE TOAST OR SANDWICH.

INGREDIENTS

2 cups raw cashews

2 to 4 tbsp canola oil, optional

salt, optional

DIRECTIONS

Place cashews into blender and press Start. Gradually increase speed to medium and blend until butter starts to form. Stop and scrape down sides as needed. Add oil and salt, if using. Replace lid and press Start. Blend on low speed and increase speed to medium speed again, blending until smooth. Transfer to an airtight container and refrigerate for up to 1 month.

Calories: 98 Fat: 8g; Chol: 0mg; Sodium: 3mg; Carb: 6g; Fiber: 1g; Protein: 3g

MAKES ABOUT 1½ CUPS

Hazelnut Cocoa Spread

POPULAR **AROUND THE WORLD**, THIS
SPREAD IS **SIMPLE** TO PREPARE, BUT WILL BE GONE IN A **FLASH**.
BE PREPARED TO MAKE MORE.

INGREDIENTS

2 cups hazelnuts, roasted, skins removed

¼ cup unsweetened cocoa powder

½ cup powdered sugar

¾ cup sweetened condensed milk

1 tsp pure vanilla extract

1 tbsp canola oil

pinch salt

DIRECTIONS

Place all ingredients into the blender in the order listed and press Start. Gradually increase speed to medium-high and blend until smooth. Transfer to an airtight container and refrigerate for up to 1 month.

Calories: 129 Fat: 9g; Chol: 1mg; Sodium: 19mg; Carb: 10g; Fiber: 2g; Protein: 3g

MAKES ABOUT 1 CUP

Homemade Peanut Butter

MAKE PEANUT BUTTER TO SUIT YOUR OWN **HAPPY PLACE**; SUPER CHUNKY, SEMI-CHUNKY, OR **SMOOTH** BEYOND SMOOTH.

INGREDIENTS

2 cups roasted peanuts

4 tbsp peanut or canola oil, optional

pinch salt, optional

DIRECTIONS

Place peanuts into the blender and add 2 tablespoons oil, if using. Press Start. Gradually increase speed to medium and blend until butter starts to form. Turn off and scrape down sides as needed. Taste and add oil and salt, if using. Press Start and gradually increase speed to medium, blending to desired consistency. Transfer to an airtight container and refrigerate for up to 1 month.

Calories: 106 Fat: 9g; Chol: 0mg; Sodium: 1mg; Carb: 4g; Fiber: 1g; Protein: 4g

MAKES ABOUT 4 CUPS

Whole Wheat Flour

USE IN YOUR FAVORITE RECIPES TO ADD
WHOLESOME INGREDIENTS INTO YOUR DAY.

INGREDIENTS

2 cups wheat berries, uncooked

DIRECTIONS

Place wheat berries into blender and press Start. Gradually increase speed to high and blend until the berries are finely ground. Store in an airtight container for up to 2 months.

Calories: 25 Fat: 0g; Chol: 0mg; Sodium: 0mg; Carb: 5g; Fiber: 1g; Protein: 1g

cook's note:

TO ENSURE A FINE FLOUR, *sift and re-grind* ANY BITS THAT REMAIN.

MAKES 2 CUPS

Brown Rice Flour

A LOVELY **GLUTEN-FREE** ALTERNATIVE.

INGREDIENTS

3 cups brown rice, uncooked

DIRECTIONS

Place rice into blender and press Start. Gradually increase speed to high and blend until the rice is finely ground. Store in an airtight container for up to 2 months.

Calories: 113 Fat: 1g; Chol: 0mg; Sodium: 0mg; Carb: 26g; Fiber: 2g; Protein: 2g

cook's note:

TO ENSURE
A FINE FLOUR,
sift and re-grind
ANY BITS THAT
REMAIN.

MAKES 2 CUPS

Oat Flour

OAT FLOUR IS **QUICK** TO MAKE AND NICE TO HAVE ON HAND TO **THICKEN** SMOOTHIES, SOUPS AND SAUCES OR TO **ADD FLAVORING** AND TEXTURE TO BAKED GOODS.

INGREDIENTS

4 cups regular or quick-cooking oats, uncooked (do not use instant oatmeal)

DIRECTIONS

Place oats into blender and press Start. Gradually increase speed to high and blend until the oats are finely ground. Store in an airtight container for up to 2 months.

Calories: 95 Fat: 2g; Chol: 0mg; Sodium: 0mg; Carb: 16g; Fiber: 3g; Protein: 4g

cook's note:

TO ENSURE A FINE FLOUR, **sift and re-grind** ANY BITS THAT REMAIN.

MAKES ABOUT 3¹/₂ CUPS

Gluten-Free Flour

GLUTEN-FREE FLOUR CAN BE AN **EXPENSIVE** ITEM TO PURCHASE AT THE GROCERY STORE. **BLEND** THIS FLOUR MIXTURE FOR PERFECT ALL-PURPOSE FLOUR.

INGREDIENTS

1½ cups brown rice, uncooked

1½ cups white rice, uncooked

¼ cup tapioca flour

1 cup potato starch

3¾ tsp xanthan gum

DIRECTIONS

Place brown and white rice into blender and press Start. Gradually increase speed to high and blend until finely ground. Add remaining ingredients and Pulse 3 to 4 times to combine. Transfer to an airtight container and store for up to 2 months.

Calories: 138 Fat: 1g; Chol: 0mg; Sodium: 41mg; Carb: 32g; Fiber: 2g; Protein: 2g

cook's note:

TO USE IN RECIPES, SUBSTITUTE **1 cup Gluten-Free Flour** PER CUP OF ALL-PURPOSE FLOUR.

MAKES 2 CUPS

Millet Flour

ANCIENT **GRAINS**, SUCH
AS MILLET, **PROVIDE FIBER** AND **NUTRIENTS** IN AN **EASY–TO–ABSORB**
FASHION. USE THIS FLOUR IN MUFFINS, BREADS AND COOKIES.

INGREDIENTS

1½ cups millet, uncooked

DIRECTIONS

Place millet into blender and press Start. Gradually increase speed to high and blend until finely ground. Store in an airtight container for up to 2 months.

Calories: 7 Fat: 1g; Chol: 0mg; Sodium: 1mg; Carb: 11g; Fiber: 2g; Protein: 2g

cook's note:

TO ENSURE
A FINE FLOUR,
sift and re-grind
ANY BITS THAT
REMAIN.

MAKES ABOUT 2¹/₄ CUPS

Quinoa Flour

TOASTING THE QUINOA SEEDS IS A **GREAT WAY** TO REMOVE THE BITTER OUTER COATING AND ADD **EXTRA FLAVOR** TO THE FLOUR.

INGREDIENTS

2 cups quinoa, uncooked, toasted

DIRECTIONS

Place quinoa into blender and press Start. Gradually increase speed to high and blend until finely ground. Store in an airtight container for up to 2 months.

Calories: 63 Fat 1g; Chol: 0mg; Sodium: 1mg; Carb: 11g; Fiber: 1g; Protein: 2g

cook's note:

TO ENSURE A FINE FLOUR, sift and re-grind ANY BITS THAT REMAIN.

MAKES 2 CUPS

Cracked Cornmeal

CRACKED CORNMEAL IS **PERFECT** FOR
COATING FISH PRIOR TO PAN-FRYING OR ADDING TO **SWEET** OR **SAVORY** BREADS.

INGREDIENTS

1½ cups popcorn kernels, unpopped

DIRECTIONS

Place popcorn into blender and press Start. Gradually increase speed to high and blend until coarsely ground. Remove any large or unblended kernels. Store in an airtight container for up to 2 months.

Calories: 68 Fat: 1g; Chol: 0mg; Sodium: 0mg; Carb: 14g; Fiber: 2g; Protein: 2g

MAKES 2 CUPS

Polenta Grains

FINELY GROUND **GRAINS** MAKE THE **PERFECT FOUNDATION** FOR YOUR FAVORITE POLENTA RECIPE.

INGREDIENTS

1½ cups popcorn kernels, unpopped

DIRECTIONS

Place popcorn into blender and press Start. Gradually increase speed to high and blend until finely ground. Remove any large or unblended kernels. Store in an airtight container for up to 2 months.

Calories: 68 Fat: 1g; Chol: 0mg; Sodium: 0mg; Carb: 14g; Fiber: 2g; Protein: 2g

MAKES ABOUT 1¼ CUPS

Grapefruit Balsamic Dressing

DRIZZLE OVER COLD CUCUMBER AND MELON SLICES
FOR A ZESTY SUMMER SALAD.

INGREDIENTS

1 pink grapefruit, peeled, pith removed

2 tbsp balsamic vinegar

½ cup sunflower oil

¼ tsp salt

DIRECTIONS

Place all ingredients into blender and press Start. Gradually increase speed to high and blend until very smooth. Refrigerate in an airtight container for up to 2 weeks. Let stand at room temperature to liquefy the oil before use.

Calories: 53 Fat: 6g; Chol: 0mg; Sodium: 28mg; Carb: 1g; Fiber: 0g; Protein: 0g

MAKES ABOUT 2¹/₂ CUPS

Tangy Tahini Dressing

A GREAT DESTINATION FOR THIS DRESSING IS
AN **ASIAN CHICKEN SALAD**, STEAMED BOK CHOI OR OTHER GREENS.

INGREDIENTS

²/₃ cup water

¹/₄ cup low-sodium soy sauce

3 tbsp lemon juice

1 clove garlic, peeled

¹/₂-inch fresh ginger root, peeled,
roughly cut

1 cup tahini (sesame seed paste)

¹/₄ tsp salt

DIRECTIONS

Place all ingredients into blender in order listed. Press Start and gradually increase speed to medium, blending until very smooth. Add water by tablespoons if a thinner dressing is desired. Refrigerate in an airtight container for up to 2 weeks.

Calories: 74 Fat: 6g; Chol: 0mg; Sodium: 138mg; Carb: 3g; Fiber: 1g; Protein: 2g

MAKES ABOUT 1¹/₂ CUPS

Orange Poppy Seed Dressing

DRIZZLE OVER BABY SPINACH LEAVES AND **TOSS** WITH MANDARIN ORANGE **SEGMENTS**, SLICED RED ONIONS AND TOASTED SESAME SEEDS.

INGREDIENTS

²/₃ **cup orange juice**

¹/₄ **cup rice wine vinegar**

¹/₂ **cup sunflower oil**

¹/₃ **cup honey**

¹/₄ **tsp salt**

1 **tbsp poppy seeds**

DIRECTIONS

Place all ingredients into blender, except poppy seeds, and press Start. Gradually increase speed to medium-low and blend until smooth. Add poppy seeds and Pulse once or twice to combine. Refrigerate in an airtight container for up to 2 weeks.

Calories: 71 Fat: 6g; Chol: 0mg; Sodium: 28mg; Carb: 6g; Fiber: 0g; Protein: 0g

MAKES ABOUT 1¹/₃ CUPS

Honey Mustard Dressing

EQUALLY AT HOME IN A SALAD OR USED AS A DIP, THIS **EASY** DRESSING IS FAIRLY **ADDICTIVE**.

INGREDIENTS

½ cup apple cider vinegar

2 tbsp Dijon mustard

¼ cup honey

½ tsp salt

½ tsp ground black pepper

¾ cup olive oil

DIRECTIONS

Place all ingredients, except oil, into blender in order listed. Press Start and blend on low until well-combined. Increase speed to medium and drizzle olive oil through the lid opening into the dressing. Continue blending until smooth. Refrigerate in an airtight container for up to 2 weeks.

Calories: 86 Fat: 8g; Chol: 0mg; Sodium: 58mg; Carb: 4g; Fiber: 0g; Protein: 0g

MAKES ABOUT 2¹/₄ CUPS

Chipotle Ranch Dressing

A BRIGHT **TWIST** ON A PERENNIAL FAVORITE.

INGREDIENTS

1 cup buttermilk

¾ cup lowfat sour cream

½ cup lowfat cottage cheese

1 canned chipotle pepper

½ tsp salt

2 tbsp flat leaf parsley, chopped

DIRECTIONS

Place all ingredients, except parsley, into blender and press Start. Pulse on medium speed until smooth, scraping down sides as needed. Add parsley and Pulse once or twice to combine. Refrigerate in an airtight container for up to 1 week.

Calories: 16 Fat: 1g; Chol: 3mg; Sodium: 96mg; Carb: 1g; Fiber: 0g; Protein: 1g

MAKES ABOUT 1½ CUPS

Creamy Gorgonzola Dressing

A LUSH, RICH DRESSING, WORTHY OF A SIMPLE HEAD OF BUTTER LETTUCE.

INGREDIENTS

½ cup whole milk

1 cup lowfat cottage cheese

¼ cup gorgonzola cheese

2 tbsp lemon juice

¼ tsp salt

¼ tsp ground black pepper

¼ cup chives, roughly cut

DIRECTIONS

Place all ingredients, except chives, into blender and press Start. Pulse on medium-low speed until smooth, scraping down sides as needed. Add chives and Pulse once or twice to combine. Refrigerate in an airtight container for up to 2 weeks.

Calories: 19 Fat: 1g; Chol: 3mg; Sodium: 94mg; Carb: 1g; Fiber: 0g; Protein: 2g

MAKES ABOUT 1¹/₃ CUPS

Lemon & Oregano Vinaigrette

A LIGHT SALAD DRESSING OR **EASY** MARINADE FOR CHICKEN OR BEEF.

INGREDIENTS

2 lemons, peeled, seeded

pinch dry mustard

2 tsp fresh oregano

½ tsp salt

½ tsp ground black pepper

¾ cup olive oil

DIRECTIONS

Place all ingredients into blender in order listed and press Start. Gradually increase speed to high, blending until very smooth. Refrigerate in an airtight container for up to 2 weeks.

Calories: 71 Fat: 8g; Chol: 0mg; Sodium: 58mg; Carb: 0g; Fiber: 0g; Protein: 0g

MAKES ABOUT 3 CUPS

Thousand Island Dressing

A CLASSIC DRESSING, LOOKING FOR A BIG WEDGE OF **ICEBERG LETTUCE** TO CALL ITS OWN. ADD **BRIGHT** PEAR TOMATOES AND GREEN ONIONS TO MAKE A **BIG STATEMENT**.

INGREDIENTS

¾ cup ketchup

¼ cup yellow onion, roughly cut

2 cloves garlic, peeled

1¾ cups lowfat mayonnaise

1 tbsp bottled chili sauce

½ tsp salt

½ tsp ground black pepper

¼ cup pickle relish

DIRECTIONS

Place all ingredients, except pickle relish, into blender in order listed. Press Start and blend on low speed until smooth. Add pickle relish and Pulse 3 times to incorporate. Refrigerate in an airtight container for up to 2 weeks.

Calories: 20 Fat: 1g; Chol: 0mg; Sodium: 210mg; Carb: 2g; Fiber: 0g; Protein: 0g

MAKES ABOUT 2 CUPS

Creamy Herb Dressing

WITH THE **TANG** OF BUTTERMILK AND CHOPPED FRESH **HERBS**, THIS DRESSING IS EASILY AT HOME OVER **GREENS** OR WHEN USED AS A **DIP** FOR BREAD OR CRACKERS.

INGREDIENTS

$2/3$ cup buttermilk

1 green onion, roughly cut

$1/3$ cup fresh parsley, roughly cut

2 tbsp fresh dill, roughly cut

3 tbsp fresh basil, roughly cut

$3/4$ tsp salt

$3/4$ tsp ground black pepper

$1/2$ cup lowfat cottage cheese

$1/2$ cup lowfat mayonnaise

$1/4$ cup apple cider vinegar

DIRECTIONS

Place all ingredients in blender in order listed. Press Start and Pulse on medium speed until well-combined. Refrigerate in an airtight container for up to 2 weeks.

Calories: 7 Fat: 0g; Chol: 1mg; Sodium: 64mg; Carb: 1g; Fiber: 0g; Protein: 0g

MAKES ABOUT 1¼ CUPS

Raspberry Vinaigrette

MIXED GREENS ARE THE PERFECT FOIL FOR THIS **FRUITY** VINAIGRETTE. THE **CHAMPAGNE** VINEGAR SOFTENS THE BITE.

INGREDIENTS

½ cup olive oil or safflower oil

¼ cup champagne vinegar

½ cup fresh raspberries

2 tbsp fresh lime juice

2 tbsp honey

½ tsp salt

½ tsp ground black pepper

DIRECTIONS

Place all ingredients into blender and press Start. Gradually increase speed to medium-low until smooth. Refrigerate in an airtight container for up to 2 weeks.

Calories: 53 Fat: 5g; Chol: 0mg; Sodium: 58mg; Carb: 1g; Fiber: 0g; Protein: 0g

MAKES ABOUT 1¹/₄ CUPS

Smoky Paprika Vinaigrette

VERSATILE ENOUGH TO **DRESS GREENS** OR
STEAMED TENDER-CRISP VEGETABLES.

INGREDIENTS

²/₃ cup red wine vinegar

1 tbsp Dijon mustard

3 tbsp lemon juice

½ shallot, peeled

1 tsp smoked paprika

½ tsp salt

½ tsp ground black pepper

1 cup olive oil

DIRECTIONS

Place all ingredients in blender in order listed and press Start.
Gradually increase speed to medium and blend until smooth.
Refrigerate in an airtight container for up to 2 weeks.

Calories: 95 Fat: 11g; Chol: 6mg; Sodium: 58mg; Carb: 0g; Fiber: 0g; Protein: 0g

MAKES ABOUT 1¹/₃ CUPS

Cool Cilantro Dressing

USE AS A DRESSING FOR SALADS OR SPOON OVER FILLED, HOT TACOS.

INGREDIENTS

¾ cup olive oil

½ cup lowfat sour cream

¼ cup fresh cilantro leaves

1 clove garlic, peeled

¼ cup lime juice

1 tbsp white wine vinegar

½ tsp salt

½ tsp ground black pepper

DIRECTIONS

Place all ingredients into blender in order listed. Press Start and gradually increase speed to medium-low. Blend until smooth. Refrigerate in an airtight container for up to 2 weeks.

Calories: 8 Fat: 9g; Chol: 2mg; Sodium: 62mg; Carb: 1g; Fiber: 0g; Protein: 0g

MAKES ABOUT 1¹/₂ CUPS

Spicy Blackberry Dressing

SPOON **LIGHTLY** OVER THIN SLICES OF MELON AND PROSCIUTTO.

INGREDIENTS

1 cup fresh blackberries

³/₄ cup olive oil

¹/₄ cup balsamic vinegar

2 tbsp honey

¹/₄ tsp bottled chili sauce

DIRECTIONS

Place all ingredients into blender and press Start. Gradually increase speed to medium and blend until smooth. Strain, if desired. Refrigerate in an airtight container for up to 2 weeks.

Calories: 67 Fat: 7g; Chol: 0mg; Sodium: 5mg; Carb: 2g; Fiber: 0g; Protein: 0g

MAKES ABOUT 1¹⁄₂ CUPS

Honeyed Champagne Vinaigrette

A **SLIGHTLY SWEET** VINAIGRETTE THAT GOES WELL WITH **PEPPERY** ARUGULA AND WILD GREENS.

INGREDIENTS

½ cup olive oil

3 tbsp honey

3 tbsp lemon juice

½ cup champagne vinegar

½ tsp salt

¼ tsp white pepper

DIRECTIONS

Place all ingredients into blender and press Start. Gradually increase speed to medium-low and blend until smooth. Refrigerate in an airtight container for up to 2 weeks.

Calories: 59 Fat: 5g; Chol: 0mg; Sodium: 58mg; Carb: 3g; Fiber: 0g; Protein: 0g

MAKES ABOUT 2 CUPS

Classic French Dressing

VERSATILE AND **BETTER THAN EVER**, HOMEMADE
FRENCH DRESSING COMPLEMENTS ALMOST ANY SALAD.

INGREDIENTS

½ cup apple cider vinegar

1 small ripe tomato, cored

½ shallot, peeled

¾ tsp ground paprika

½ tsp salt

½ tsp celery seed

1 cup olive oil

DIRECTIONS

Place all ingredients into the blender and press Start. Gradually
increase speed to medium-low and blend until smooth. Refrigerate in
an airtight container for up to 2 weeks.

Calories: 80 Fat: 9g; Chol: 0mg; Sodium: 48mg; Carb: 0g; Fiber: 0g; Protein: 0g

MAKES ABOUT 1¹/₂ CUPS

Italian Herbed Dressing

ROBUST **HERBS** AND GARLIC STAR IN THIS
VIBRANT DRESSING.

INGREDIENTS

¹/₂ cup red wine vinegar

2 tbsp water

2 cloves garlic, peeled

3 tbsp onion, chopped

1 tsp each: dried parsley, dried
basil, dried oregano

¹/₂ tsp salt

¹/₂ tsp ground black pepper

1 cup olive oil

DIRECTIONS

Place all ingredients into blender and press Start. Gradually increase
speed to medium-low and blend until smooth. Refrigerate in an airtight
container for up to 2 weeks.

Calories: 97 Fat: 10g; Chol: 0mg; Sodium: 58mg; Carb: 0g; Fiber: 0g; Protein: 0g

Index

Nuts for Berry Bars,
page 101

Index

Index

Index

Index